NEW TECHNOLOGIES AND PROFESSIONAL COMMUNICATIONS IN EDUCATION

Occasional Paper 13

New Technologies and Professional Communications in Education

Edited by
David Smith

National Council for Educational Technology

Published and distributed by the
National Council for Educational Technology
3 Devonshire Street, London W1N 2BA

First published 1988

ISBN 0 86184-184-0
ISSN 0307-952X

BL British Library Cataloguing in Publication Data

New technologies and professional communications in
    education. —
    (Occasional paper/NCET, ISSN 0307-952X; 13)
    1. Great Britain. Education. Effects of technological
    innovation
    I. Smith, David   II. National Council for Educational
    Technology
    370'.941

    ISBN 0-86184-184-0

Typeset by WHM Photosetting, 33 The Market, Greenwich

Printed in Great Britain by
Blackfords of Cornwall, St Austell

Contents

Foreword

What struck me forcibly about the papers which make up this book is that, together, they provide me with evidence and argument, from a variety of standpoints, of something I have suspected, indeed warned enthusiastically about, ever since someone showed me that a personal computer could receive and transmit text and graphics. I foresaw changes in the patterns of communication which would undermine the most basic structures of our education and training system. It hasn't happened — yet — but these papers are reports from the front which suggest the sappers are already under the foundations.

What unites them for me is that they report not so much on the technology as on the effects it has on those who use it — the 'message' of the medium in McLuhan's terms, or the hidden curriculum if you prefer.

Julia Cooper and Kate Bainbridge (and colleagues) argue from extended analogies, of the business world and private transport systems respectively, to indicate the kinds of structural changes we might expect in education and training. Neither is uncritically enthusiastic about what they foresee. 'Power to the People' (which is what some promise from unrestricted access to information and instruction) is an attractive slogan but a difficult principle to live by, particularly if you are charged by (some of) the people with the responsibilities of a teacher.

It is the shifting of 'The power to do for oneself' — and the resulting changes in interpersonal relationships — which several of the authors find of interest. Ros Keep, and Tony Scott in a different way, see the new technologies as potentially establishing a redefined sense of professional identity among teachers. David Smith predicts the need for tertiary education to move into the marketplace. Gordon Bell and Susan Dennis expect that new technologies will close the gaps between researchers and practitioners in education and training. And so on.

Many of the papers speculate as to what may happen. The case studies offer evidence that it does happen. Jane Cox and Valerie Campbell have witnessed the qualitative changes in self confidence and personality, and the exciting progress in communication and interpersonal skills which leaners can make when challenged to use the new information and communication technologies for themselves. David McConnell has noted a new democracy among participants when seminars are computer conferences held over extended periods instead of the intimidating performances that I remember from university days.

I hope other readers will gather from these papers the same sense of cautious excitement that they conveyed to me and will take pleasure in detecting from them the hidden curriculum of the new technologies in Education and Training.

Clive Neville
NCET Programme Manager

Preface

This book has its origins in a series of discussions and seminars held under the aegis of the National Foundation for Educational Research (NFER) and the Council for Educational Technology (CET) during the spring and early summer of 1987, with some support from the Microelectronics Education Support Unit (MESU — now amalgamated with CET to form NCET). These first meetings spawned an informal group of educators interested in the application of new communications technologies to education. This group grew rapidly during 1987, due largely to the energy and enthusiasm of Tom Holloway, on secondment from IBM. In growing, the group made contact with others who had similar interests. What was originally a matter of minority interest became apparent as a substantial field of educational development.

The papers in this book represent the development of ideas within this growing community of educators. They vary in length, depth of treatment, context, style and in all manner of other ways. The book is not intended to be an academic treatise, but a 'snapshot album'. The papers attempt to deal with issues arising from a groundswell of interest in the potential of new Information Technologies for enhancing professional communications at many levels of the education system. It is a contribution to a continuing process of discussion and debate.

We hope that the ideas presented here will prove to be relevant and valuable in the context of education for the 'Information Age'.

Introduction: computer mediated communications technologies in education

David Smith
Centre for Evaluation of Information Technology (CITE);
National Foundation for Educational Research

During the past three or four years, educational computer applications have finally moved out of the era of electronic programmed learning and statistical number-crunching. The computer and its friends-and-relations are increasingly seen as general purpose tools, rather than dedicated (and limited) devices. Spreadsheets, database packages and word processors have almost revolutionised some aspects of educational administration, whilst 'tool' uses for computers currently represent some of the most promising avenues for classroom-based curriculum development.

One aspect of the growing 'tool' use of the computer, which could have massively important implications for the educational system, is in communications. The use of the computer workstation as a communications device is nothing new in industry and commerce, and in some universities and colleges, but most educational computer users are only just beginning to explore what is, to them at least, an entirely new medium.

Probably the best established computer-based communications technology is viewdata. This undoubtedly owes a great deal to the work over many years of the Council for Educational Technology's Videotex Unit (now disbanded). There are numerous instances of innovative curricular use of viewdata systems and particularly of British Telecom's Prestel system.

Apart from the public viewdata services, The Times Network Systems (TTNS) have provided educators with a variety of on-line services, including bulletin-boards, databases and electronic mail. The applications of these systems in the curriculum are also well documented. Less well documented but potentially very valuable to such developments as open learning are computer conferencing systems. Despite their popularity with computer 'buffs', conferencing systems have yet to establish themselves in the UK, though their use is beginning to take off.

Despite the recent rapid growth of computer-based communications systems in the UK (see, for example, Julia Cooper's paper in this volume), their user-bases are all quite limited when compared with the numbers of educators who might be expected to find uses for new communications media. Why this might be is a matter for conjecture, since there is little reliable research in this field. Reasons could range from non-availability of hardware (British primary schools had one computer for about 100 pupils in 1985/86) to lack of appropriate professional training. We simply do not know.

In any case, in an educational system which seems to have been plagued with solutions in search of problems, we have to face the question whether these new communications systems actually meet any real needs. This, too, is difficult to answer directly. There are two factors which must be taken into account here:

— ways in which new technologies may help us to do our present work more efficiently or effectively;

— ways in which new technologies may enable us to do things which were previously impossible.

Both of these issues are dealt with in the collection of writings which figure in this book.

Our prime concern, as committed educators, is that educational considerations should be foremost when new technological systems are designed and implemented. Indeed, it has become almost a pious incantation that 'needs' should determine products. So they should — in an ideal world. But we live in a world which is far from ideal and it is only rarely that we enjoy the luxury of specifying devices on the basis of educational need. Furthermore, our awareness of possibilities often only stems from seeing something and wondering what it could do in our case.

This is not to suggest that education has to play a passive role, absorbing whatever manufacturers care to sell, irrespective of need. But we need to start in the real world. Many, if not most, advances in the educational applications of new technologies have come from creative professionals who have been inspired by even very limited aspects of the technology, rather than through the prior considerations of 'procurement committees'!

Not too far into the future, there is the prospect of a new generation of advanced computers which will incorporate full read-write multimedia and wide-based communications facilities. The (temporarily stalled) European DELTA programme envisages that, by the mid 1990s, the desk-top workstation will have the processing power of 200 of today's PC machines and will have access to satellite communications links. How will we respond to the possibilities, challenges and dangers inherent in such devices?

The answer must surely be 'not very effectively' if we turn away from the admittedly imperfect systems currently at our disposal in vain attempts to design 'perfect' systems from first principles. The process of learning to think creatively about the coming generation of computer technology must start now (or should have started some time ago!). The more people we have applying their professional intuition and creativity to extant systems, then the greater leverage we may hope to exert on the directions which the suppliers of the technologies may take. We must be able to identify and articulate our needs — or somebody else will do it for us.

A number of superficially attractive developments have already been proposed by business people, often with very little educational expertise. In the USA, for instance, Jack Taub, the originator of the database system 'The Source' has announced plans for what he calls 'The Educational Utility'. He calls for private investors to install and service computers in each school. The computers would be linked by satellite to a central database of software, textbooks, etc (Fig 1). Taub's plan leaves most of the educational questions untouched and, for that reason alone, it would be foolish for educators to fail to take seriously his chances of installing his system. If he does succeed (and he might), it will be up to educational professionals to make the system work. And that is equally true of much more socially-oriented developments.

The writings in this book represent attempts to begin the process of exploration. Some authors describe experiments with classroom practice, some function at a more theoretical level. All share a common concern that technology should be under human control, and not vice-versa.

References
1. Kania, H (1984), *Prestel for People*, CET, London.
2. Kaye, A (1987), Introducing Computer Mediated Communications into a Distance Education System, *Canadian Journal of Educational Communications* 16, 2.
3. Kaye, A (1987), On-line Services for Schools: an appraisal, in Jones, A and Scrimshaw, P (eds), *Computers in Education 5-13*, Open University Press, Milton Keynes.
4. DES Statistical Bulletin 18/86, *Results of the Survey of Microcomputers etc in Schools — Autumn 1985*, Department of Education and Science, London.
5. European Commission (1987), *Development of European Learning through Technological Advance: Initial Studies*, Les Editions du Logical d'Enseignement, Paris.
6. Middleton, T (1986), The Educator – Utility, *American Educator 10*, 4 14-25.

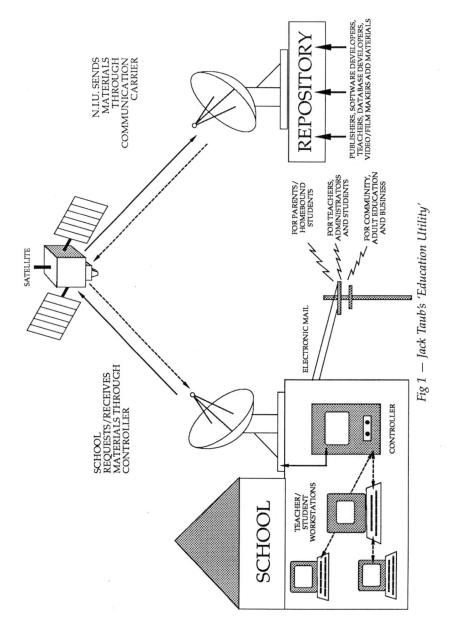

Fig 1 — Jack Taub's 'Education Utility'

PART I

Thinking Ahead

The contributions in this section deal in different ways with the future development of electronic communications. They don't pretend to be deep futurological analyses, but rather 'think-pieces', addressed to the question 'what if . . .?' Julia Cooper and Ros Keep offer optimistic views of ways in which the new communications technologies can serve teachers and students. Kate Bainbridge and her colleagues are more sombre, looking through the 'hype' to some of the potential dangers of computer-mediated communications. David Smith is also sceptical, but this time about the cultural jingoism of the 'Information Age'; he asks whether there might not be some surprises in store for the 'developed nations'.

1. Do you read me?

Julia Cooper
British Telecom

The use of electronic communications in business affects the flow of information around an organisation, by increasing the quality of information available and the speed with which it can be accessed. These are the objective, observable effects. But what of the subjective effects, upon the user? Most formal communication within an organisation seems to be vertical but informal channels of communication, which circumvent hierarchical structures, are often more powerful. What are the implications of electronic communications for power and control within organisations? Does it reinforce or subvert hierarchies; help or hinder effective decision-making; strengthen or weaken human networks?

The ability to distribute an electronic message to a large number of recipients simultaneously and to forward a message received by oneself, to any number of colleagues, can widen the audience to potentially relevant snippets. The ease with which we can disseminate copies of original messages with comments appended, to third parties, can aid delegation. The ease of instant reply to queries serves to speed up decision-making. The effect on quality of decision-making can be ambivalent however. It is often more prudent to give a quick acknowledgement, encapsulating our initial reaction, followed by a more measured response, later. Moreover, effective decision-making is not enhanced by the quantity of information at our disposal but the quality of it. The impression of decentralisation of responsibilities can be countered by the possibility of control at the top being strengthened by increased ease of contact of subordinates by superiors, whether they are in the office or out of it, and improved channels of reporting back. In either case, the busy manager can certainly increase her efficiency by reducing the need to wait for physical meetings and the time wasted in making unsuccessful telephone calls.

If electronic mailbox numbers are widely known, it becomes much easier for a subordinate to contact a superior directly, bypassing intermediaries such as a secretary. In one local education authority, any teacher, or indeed pupil, could mail the Chief Education Officer, whose number they would find on an electronic directory of E-mail users. The fact that his number is there, probably indicates that he is an approachable person who wants to be accessible in any case but, even so, the medium facilitates his aim and, on the particular E-mail system in question, one cannot send an anonymous message!

The medium also encourages informality of address and a familiarity and spontaneity of style that tends to strengthen human communicativeness — if not human communication!

For example, first name terms are widely used, jokes and light asides exchanged, between people who have never met (and perhaps hope they never will meet!). This tends to enrich and personalise exchanges which might otherwise have remained basic, devoid of the extra signals humans can give each other on a medium which has combined the characteristics of both the written and the spoken word.

It can even sometimes demonstrate a levelling effect, helping overcome barriers of age, colour, accent or disability. We can even make new friends on E-mail — witness the Cambridge student who 'met' her American husband this way; not to mention the use Parisian 'ladies of the night' make of Teletel (the French equivalent of Prestel)!

There are, however, some communicative signals which cannot be transmitted electronically, such as body language and tone of voice. Coupled with the use of perfunctory one-line messages, there is the possibility of mistaking brevity for brusqueness. This can be compounded by the quick reply, viz: 'OK if you are willing so am I', to a question which the sender has subsequently forgotten! (Telecom Gold does allow us to append an answer to the original query and mail them both back to the sender. A sensible precaution is to use the carbon copy facility, too.)

Some regular users of E-mail would add the 'reply requested' and 'acknowledgement requested' facilities of Gold to the downside of the equation, in that these attempts to force a reply and that the sender knows as soon as you have read the message could be viewed as an invasion of privacy. But they pale into insignificance when compared to the persistent ringing of a telephone.

I wonder in this context whether, in the eyes of more traditional office workers, the E-mail item may lack the binding import of message committed to paper? In human communication, the subjective credibility of a source of information is more important than the person's expertise — could the medium, in this case, detract from the content of the message?

Turning to the linguistic changes perceived by some users: use of E-mail seems to mitigate against careful, well-structured prose, unless the user has sent a pre-prepared, word-processed document (readers of this article may well wonder whether electronics could render the style even more unmanageable!). It is so easy to send an amendment if we make a mistake.

(Much easier, in fact, than to attempt to master the archaic on-line editor, thoughtfully provided by Telecom Gold.) Difficulty in sending accented characters is also a drawback for the modern linguist.

Are the technologists then, really helping us to communicate better? Are their developments enabling us to access and shape information more readily, subverting hierarchies as we go? As with all aspects of new technologies, capabilities exceed the ability of the ordinary user to conceive of how to implement them, usefully, in his own working environment. This must have been true of the telephone and the word processor, which are now commonplace. I think the same will apply to electronic mail.

Extant systems still display an element of user-hostility which some would compare unfavourably with using pen and paper or the telephone; note some of the error messages confronting the Telecom Gold user, viz 'illegal-tree-name' and 'Not found in segment directory. OPEN JULSEG ONE WORD (16)', not to mention the esoteric gems appearing on our screens, courtesy of the Packet Switch Stream Network. 'CLR DER!' it shrieks angrily at us, to which we happily reply 'Log off'. Occasional line noise (for those of us in education not blessed with private lines) which sends control codes down the line after our packets, aborting messages as we look on in helpless wonder, is seen as a challenge to those of us of pioneering spirit but may be off-putting to the less committed novice.

However, I am convinced that the telecommunications industry will make a quantum leap in quality of service and user friendliness of systems, as digital exchanges spread nationally and the X400 standard is implemented.

British Telecom is committed to adhering to international standards. If other national PTTs follow suit, the global village will be one step closer and we may not only be discussing the scaling of hierarchical boundaries but of national ones. Users of the International Packet Switch Stream Network will have noted the recent additions of Chile and Hungary to the fold and Dialcom Licences are being sold to an increasing number of operators from Scandinavia to Singapore. We can only hope that international telecomms will help transcend the artificial barriers constructed by competing political systems.

Already, school children are showing us the way. There are projects linking schools in Devon and Tasmania, Cambridge and the US, and Britain and France on the Times Network. Children are building cultural understanding, using a form of direct contact which was not possible before. Pupils in Bologna were surprised to know that their counterparts in Canada were pleased that a new supermarket had eliminated their former need to reach shops by crossing a lake by boat. Israeli children were confounded by a description of a kibbutz, sent to them from a Japanese group. They responded with a rapid clarification of life on a kibbutz as they saw it! Devon children were happily communicating about football, when they realised that the rules the Tasmanian kids played by were completely different!

I will leave you to draw your own conclusions as to the implications of this type of activity for those who have been accustomed to mediating or controlling the flow of information and access to it. It would be premature and naive to herald a new era of 'power to the people' with micros, modems and telephone lines (which excludes the third world immediately). Information is created by people, some of whom will undoubtedly use data communications and storage techniques to deny access to information whilst centralising control and storage of it. However, I would prefer to end on an optimistic note, which demands that we make an effort to come to terms with and familiarise ourselves with the technology, in order to educate the young, to increase efficiency in the workplace and improve the quality of our human communications in general.

2. Teacher centred learning

Ros Keep
European Educational Software

This article is Ros Keep's own work and does not necessarily reflect the policies of E2S.

Teachers' Centres can be wonderfully stimulating places: they are centres for learning new skills, keeping in touch with new methods, sharing experiences, looking at new resources (as well as catching up with existing ones) and for keeping in contact with people and events. They can provide a focus for teacher-based activities, from setting up groups to discuss specific problems to just meeting for a chat. But even where Teachers' Centres exist and are accessible to local teachers, they are not always used to their full potential.

Imagine a Teachers' Centre that you don't have to travel to but can attend at any time of the night or day. Where you can guarantee that if the person you want to speak to is not there, at least you know he or she will receive a message. Where you can meet experts from all over the country, ask questions on a one-to-one basis or in an open forum. Where you can go to find out what you need to know — not what some tutor thinks you should know — from other experienced professional people. Where you can take copies (legally!) of resources and worksheets for use in class.

It would be an 'Electronic Teachers' Centre' but set up in such a friendly, comfortable and familiar environment that the technology did not obstruct the user. It would be easy to enter and clear in use, with all the links to existing services — Prestel, TTNS, Telecom Gold, NERIS, etc — invisible to the user.

The situation would be that of a well-organised, well-run Centre but, unlike most Centres, it would have almost unlimited resources. There would be different 'rooms' for different areas of interest and different activities. Most rooms would be open to all, although there should also be a facility for closed membership groups. There would be a message service, a print shop, a library, a resources room and a coffee room.

Messages
The Centre would have a comprehensive messaging system, not just for one-to-one contacts but also for one-to-many and group-to-group contact. It is often very difficult to contact advisers and other teaching colleagues by 'phone: electronic mail offers a guarantee that your message will be received, and the facility to collect and respond to messages at any time of the night or day. But E-mail can do something for communication which cannot be done in any other ways: it can offer a quick response to a message aimed at an

unknown audience. By means of a noticeboard, a teacher can contact others with similar interests without first having their names and addresses.

In the Electronic Teachers' Centre, personal messages would be collected or sent from the 'reception' area using BT Gold, TTNS or Prestel. There would also be a noticeboard in every room on which anyone could leave messages for others with similar interests to respond. The noticeboard would, of course, be open to view by all unless the room is one which is kept 'locked' for members only. There should also be a general noticeboard, perhaps in the coffee room or reception area, for more general messages. This noticeboard system would allow users to make new contacts, perhaps to set up new groups, and to make suggestions for Centre events.

Gathering information
Information comes in many forms and from many directions. One of the major tasks of the Centre would be to provide information for users in an accessible way. This could be achieved in many cases by links with existing information providers on established systems such as NERIS, ECCTIS and the subject associations.

For major interests, the user could request information on particular issues to be sent directly to his or her mailbox. This would result in a message giving the title of the document or type of material and details of where it can be found or how it can be obtained. One-off searches would be run from the Library: the Centre's own files would be searched and suggestions would be made as to where the user could look for further information. Classroom resources would be collected from the Resources Room. These could be worksheets, computer software or ideas sent in by other teachers or groups and perhaps supplied by NERIS.

When information is found, it could be printed out (via the Print Room), copied on to a disk or saved into a 'Notepad', along with personal notes, which can later be saved and used in a word processor.

A potentially important (and mostly untapped) source of information is other professionals and it is this source which can be more fully explored within such a system. Users, as individuals or groups, should be able to send information in a number of forms to the Library or the Resources Room to be added to the Centre's files. But some of the most useful and interesting information is not written anywhere and this can only be found by discussion with other professional people.

Open learning
The Centre could provide teachers with an opportunity for *real* open learning in which they choose not only the time and place for their studies,

but also the content: they study what is important to them, not what a course demands. The Centre could run courses and seminars, perhaps with an 'outside speaker' to lead discussion and provide information. These would be run along the lines of existing computer conferencing techniques or as a real-time 'chat' facility, with questions and comments either being open to all, or directed at a particular person. Sessions could be set up by users, or by the Centre's Leader (or 'moderator'). If the session is of the conference type, there is of course no need for 'delegates' to go on-line simultaneously: they can read the comments and add their own at any time. If it is of the 'chat' type, it should still be possible for those interested to download a copy of proceedings of the session and perhaps request a follow-up.

The above scenario contains little that is new: many of the facilities do already exist on established systems. But they are not easy to find and are often not easy to use. This outline shows how existing facilities could be pulled together and 'front-ended' to provide a really comfortable environment designed specifically for teachers which would enable them to exploit all the facilities available without being a technical genius. It may not suit everyone, and it is certainly not intended to replace Teachers' Centres, but it might give some teachers a better opportunity to 'meet', discuss issues, ask for help and advice, find information, swap materials and resources, attend courses — in fact do almost everything they could do at the local Teachers' Centre. And there is no reason why other professionals might not also find it useful.

3. Fair shares of a new cake: the evolution of tertiary education in the age of communications

David Smith
Centre for Evaluation of Information Technology in Education (CITE): National Foundation for Educational Research

Introduction

In any competitive situation, it is a dangerous fallacy to proceed on the assumption that one's competitors will inevitably adopt whatever strategy is most favourable to oneself. Sadly, however, much public discussion in technologically and economically 'advanced' countries about the future pattern and direction of economic development appears to rest on fallacies of this sort. As these nations evolve (or decline!) towards 'de-industrialised' or 'post-industrial' status, it appears to be regarded as axiomatic that today's less developed countries will remain contented to concentrate their economies around agriculture, mineral extraction and production-oriented manufacturing industries, whilst the economic focus of the de-industrialising countries adjusts itself towards emphasis on the provision of knowledge-based services.

It appears most unlikely that developing countries will, or indeed can, remain content to be clients for information services in a world where, to an ever-increasing extent, information is power. This is a sphere where a powerful technological imperative is operative and where decision-making is likely to be rooted as much in political as in economic considerations. One has only to recall the mushrooming of national airlines in recent decades and the eventual collapse of the profitability of many air services, for a sight of one potential scenario for the evolution of traded information services.

There is an enormous literature in economics concerning the international division of labour and innovation, trade and product cycles. The advantage of many developing countries in production-oriented manufacturing industries is now abundantly clear and a matter of very great concern to those countries who find their industrial base unable to survive in the face of a combination of massive investment in modern manufacturing technology, low production overheads, low expenditure on research and development and relatively docile labour forces.

Many observers appear to feel unusually confident in looking to knowledge-based activities to revitalise the economic base of post-industrial societies. There is often a conscious or unconscious tendency towards what might be called 'economic Darwinism'. Thus, the classification of economic types in Bell's (1) discussion of the social aspects of the information society may be held to imply an orderly and necessary evolutionary sequence through which development must proceed. This can be at best little more than a comforting illusion and at worse dangerous self-deception. There are people alive today in rapidly advancing societies whose first sight of the wheel was on an aircraft. The children and grandchildren of these same people could be actively engaged in indigenous knowledge industries. The pressures acting on tertiary education in the near future will not be the need to keep 'one jump ahead' of the opposition (who are, considerately, doing everything we want them to), but rather the need to come to terms with a richer and more complex pattern of international trade in which many traditional assumptions are no longer valid.

The natural history of invention
Gosling (2), speaking of a 'Natural History of Invention', argued that there is a tendency for industrial and technological development to follow a logistic curve (Fig 3.1) over its life span. Economists will object that this is simply

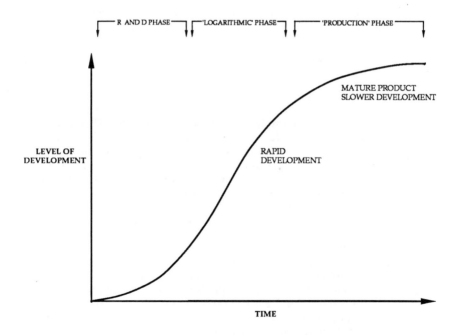

Fig 3.1 — Gosling's 'The Natural History of an Invention'

a trivialised product cycle model but it nevertheless provides a good format for non-technical discussion. The complexities underlying the model may be explored rigorously elsewhere. The production phase is the region in the curve where the advantages of developing countries are most marked for a wide range of goods. Exceptions to this generalisation may be found in the case of industries, processes or products where the capital, skill or knowledge content at the production phase is very high. For many classes of goods, however, the advantage of the developing countries is clearly marked and, in the case of rapidly developing industries, this point may be reached even before R & D costs are adequately covered. The pace of maturation of industries and processes can only accelerate as production-phase countries acquire skilled, educated and disciplined workforces, and as sophisticated robot plants (with the capacity for nigh instantaneous product changes) are installed. If this process is accepted as inevitable, then it is clear that it must be anticipated by massive marketing efforts during the 'pre-production' phase of the cycle. Such a strategy would incidentally imply a shift of emphasis towards marketing in tertiary education, in order to supply adequately and appropriately trained manpower.

One 'defensive' strategy which post-industrial countries might adopt is to concentrate on mature high-technology, high added-value industries, where the entry cost for new 'club members' is prohibitive. These industries are 'human capital intensive', a fact which has a variety of implications for education systems.

Another potential defensive strategy is the promotion of a massive R & D effort on an intensive scale to ensure the replacement of technologies, products and processes before they reach maturity (Fig 3.2). This strategy may be seen in the drive for fifth generation computers, where the prospect of Japanese advantage has stimulated near panic in some quarters (3). A problem with this approach is that its success will depend on the ready availability of a good supply of state-of-the-art trained scientists and technologists, and a flexible workforce, able to respond to new conditions. Both of these will require educational and training systems which are highly efficient and effective and responsive to new demands.

The knowledge industry
Knowledge-based services have always been economically significant, even if only marginally so. Medicine, legal services, financial services, insurance, education and so on all fall into this category, as well as the range of services supplied by what Galbraith (4) called the 'Technostructure'. It is, however, only recently that economists have developed analytic tools for estimating the true magnitude and value of knowledge and information services within developed economies and there are as yet few reliable

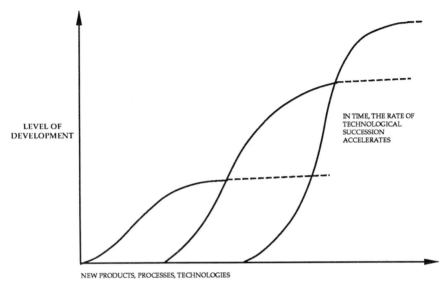

LEVEL OF
DEVELOPMENT

IN TIME, THE RATE OF
TECHNOLOGICAL
SUCCESSION
ACCELERATES

NEW PRODUCTS, PROCESSES, TECHNOLOGIES

TIME

Fig 3.2 — Technological succession

estimates of the international significance of traded knowledge-based services, except in certain specialised sectors.

Although some of the grosser assumptions about the advent of the 'Information Society' have been challenged (5), the trend in advanced economies has already proceeded to the point that a considerable percentage of the economically active population of the USA (and other countries to a lesser extent) are engaged in creating and processing information, and are using advanced automated technologies in so doing. At the same time, advances in telecommunications technologies such as high bandwidth cable systems, direct broadcasting by satellite and the whole paraphernalia of what has been rather clumsily labelled 'compunications' (computer-based communications systems) provide the means by which workforces may be dispersed. It is no longer necessary for a significant majority of people to be tied down to factories or offices. Increasingly, they can work from home or in small groups, using modern telecommunications systems to access remote computers, to address databases or even to oversee completely automated process operations.

It is this dramatic expansion in the capabilities of communications systems which provides the key to a potential shift in the world balance of traded information services. It has already been suggested above that countries will not wish to be excluded from access to services and facilities which are inextricably linked with real political and economic power. At present, less wealthy countries are limited by the high entry costs attendant on the establishment of hardware and human resources infrastructures from direct participation in computer-based knowledge 'industries', and related problems may even affect some wealthier countries (6, 7, 8). With the development of routes of access to powerful remote computing facilities, some (but not by any means all) countries will be able to enter the knowledge market through selective, and in some cases relatively small, investment in human capital. Indeed, there is already evidence for the rapid development of what has been called (9) 'Sunshine Computing'.

In the short term, obvious entry points will be into the provision of mature services, such as computer programming, systems analysis and software engineering. But as the state of the art develops and IKBS technology advances, we will also see national initiatives in the production of specialised expert systems, for example in the realm of regional market intelligence. Some countries, such as India, with surpluses of highly educated manpower are well placed to make this kind of step.

It seems clear that it will be necessary in future to recognise and plan for the existence of an international division of labour in information and knowledge-based services, closely analogous to that which now obtains for other industries (10). This new fact of economic life will inevitably affect the economies of post-industrial nations in ways which may prove to be even more deleterious than the effects of international competition within production-based manufacturing industries, unless appropriate infra-structural adjustments are made to anticipate and forestall such effects.

The role of education
The changes which have been referred to above cannot and should not be resisted by discrimination against developing countries. What we are observing now and what we are likely to observe during the next few years amounts to a major adjustment in the equilibrium of the world economic system. Modern technologies enable us to envisage the coming reality of the age-old dream of societies where misery and drudgery are minimised, if not entirely eliminated. Our perspective must extend beyond local advantage to encompass a new world-picture. It is already clear from Japanese fifth generation initiatives that technological innovation in the field of Information Technology requires R & D efforts which are beyond the resources even of most wealthy advanced nations (a trend obvious also

in such fields as aerospace industries). There is the early indication of a trend towards multinational collaboration but the cost of participation in this process will mean at the very least heavy investment in human capital and this in turn means attention to education.

This is not a Utopian vision. It is unrealistic to predict the eventual abandonment of all economic competition or a gradual relapse into computer-assisted noble savagery! Even though a convergence of R & D efforts may be predicted, there will undoubtedly be fierce competition in the markets for knowledge-based services and products. Innovators will still be able to enjoy 'technology-gap' advantages but such advantages will be increasingly short-lived. As long ago as 1965, Bagrit (11) was able to point out that the time-lag taken for a technological advantage to be eroded had been greatly reduced by high speed communications and world-wide training in science and technology. This is doubly true now and in the forseeable future. It is doubly probable for knowledge and information services.

It would appear that the so-called post-industrial nations must concentrate their efforts on maintaining a steady flow of new products and knowledge-based services, and the effective and rapid exploitation of the ever-shortening advantage which this confers in the market place. In order for this to be achieved, however, workers at all levels, from the highest to the lowest, must become effective in new roles as quickly as possible and at optimum cost. This demands a degree of flexibility which most current educational systems cannot offer and it is abundantly clear that great adjustments in educational systems will be required. In particular, 'front-end' models of education must be supplanted by structures more appropriate to lifelong continuing education and retraining.

As Smith and Sage (12) have argued, there will be a need for the elaboration of 'computer literacy' education at all levels, together with a concentration on transferable process-related skills rather than short-lived specialist knowledge. Future occupational mobility, and the training on which it will depend, will demand sound foundations of transferable skills, knowledge and attitudes. Modern information technology offers a host of potential solutions to the various problems implicit in these needs. Indeed, it is quite likely that the application of modern technology and advances in distance learning techniques will greatly reduce, or at least radically alter, the role of traditional formal institutions of tertiary education. In anticipation of these changes, there is much need for research into ways in which the variety of available technology and the range of feasible learning environments can contribute to specific curricular experiences.

It is possible to envisage a number of ways in which tertiary education institutions may adapt to meet the new challenges facing them.

1. Colleges and other institutions must develop rapid response strategies for course design development and implementation. This will necessitate a prospective rather than reactive approach to the identification of education and training needs. College staff will need to work closely with employers, organisations and trades unions to anticipate future developments.

2. Resource sharing, particularly in relation to IT-based learning media, will become more prominent. Increasingly, institutions will integrate into an electronic resource net. Databases such as NERIS may be significant early steps in this process.

3. There will be an accelerating trend towards internationalisation of tertiary education, in the light of pressures towards international labour mobility. Courses and certification procedures will be harmonised, to permit flexibility of training and personal development.

4. In train with the moves towards harmonised certifications, there will be a gathering momentum in the development of open learning systems. This will mean that institutions will place less and less reliance on a 'captive' clientele and will adopt the role of facilitators and resource providers in autonomously determined personalised learning programmes.

5. There will be the need for continuing programmes of staff upgrading. These too will use open learning systems, so that tutors and other teaching staff will gain state-of-the-art experience *as learners* within the systems which they are supporting professionally. This will serve to reduce the gulf between teachers and taught.

6. Some element of 'future study' will occupy a prominent place in all curricula, and in the routine administration of colleges and other centres of tertiary education.

In the course of these institutional adjustments, it is inevitable that tertiary education systems will acquire considerable expertise and knowledge in the realm of instructional design based on new technologies. It is possible to see this as the basis of an internationally traded market for educational services within the context of the 'knowledge industry'. Given the relatively advanced status of educational knowledge and experience in many developed countries and the likely expansion of this knowledge in the forseeable future, the conditions exist for the establishment of a technology-gap trade between developed and less developed countries. Unlike the classic strategy of sending their young people abroad for education (with the attendant risks of 'brain drains' and 'cultural contamination'), or educating them at home within a system constrained by an inadequate infrastructure (6), the purchase of educational services would allow developing countries to determine fairly precisely the pace and direction of their investment in human capital.

Mabogunje (13) pointed to the enormous and apparently insuperable problems which many developing countries face in attaining the level of material development achieved in already developed nations. But this assumes the cultural Darwinist approach which has already been criticised above. Countries do not need to shadow each others' patterns of cultural and economic evolution, and there is no imperative which dictates the necessity of passing through a sequence of technological phases. Such an idea derives from nineteenth century attempts to establish by 'scientific' means the superiority of Europeans and to affirm their special status as the pinnacle of organic evolution. Instead, as Mabogunje himself pointed out, there is the possible development strategy of abandoning the conventional sequence and settling down to fashion a new goal more consistent with local resource endowment and sociocultural disposition. With an adequate technostructure, access to modern information technology and 'custom-built' educational systems related to national development strategies, this may be a viable option.

The burgeoning of modern telecommunications and information technology offers opportunities in two directions. Firstly, it provides post-industrial societies with frameworks for economic retrenchment. Secondly, it gives many (but not all) developing countries a new hope for access to the social, cultural and material benefits of a new economic order.

Conclusion
If physical communications has been the key to the establishment of the present economic order (14), then advanced technology will be the medium through which a new equilibrium is attained. We cannot yet know what form this equilibrium will take, nor yet the status which our own societies will achieve within it. We find it all too easy to assume that things as they are now represent some ideal system and all too easy to forget that today's dominant society was yesterday's developing country. We have seen Japan rise to become one of the dominant technological powers on earth. We have seen Singapore change from a trading emporium to a major manufacturing society. We have seen the eclipse of the British Empire and the gestation of the European Community. The future pattern of trade and of economic influence and power is uncertain — even unpredictable.

One thing *can* be predicted. In the future, the creation of wealth will depend on the creation and exploitation of knowledge. The power of the computer and the capacity of modern information and communications technology for making this power available will free large numbers of people throughout the world for imaginative thinking. The result will be a release of creative energy through which not only processes and products, but also services and even whole industries, will evolve, flourish and become extinct at a rate undreamed of before in history. To cope with this rapid technological change and the social changes which will go with it, world-wide changes in educational systems will be demanded. It is too late now to be contemplating minor adjustments. Tertiary education must plan boldly for the challenges of the age of communications. The alternative is technological, economic and cultural oblivion.

References

1. Bell, D (1980), The Social Framework of the Information Society, in Forester, T (ed), *The Microelectronics Revolution*, Blackwell, Oxford, pp500-549.
2. Gosling, W (1981), *The Kingdom of Sand*, CET, London.
3. Alvey, J (1982), *A Programme for Advanced Information Technology* (The Report of the Alvey Committee), HMSO, London.
4. Galbraith, J K (1967), *The New Industrial State*, Houghton-Mifflin, Boston.
5. Wiio, O A (1985), Information Economy and the Information Society, *Media in Education and Development 18*, 4 187-191.
6. Jamshidi, M, Malek-Zaverei, M and Vakilzadeh, I (1979), Problems of Automatic Control Education in Developing Countries, *Automatika 15*, 105-112.
7. el Sayed Noor, A (1983), Computer Based Information Systems Education in the Arab World, *Computer Education 7*, 109-120.
8. Goreham, G A (1985), The Effects of Computers and the Computer Industry on the Development of Third World Nations, *Computers and Social Science 1*, 141-147.
9. Large, P (1986), Sunshine Computing, *The Guardian*.
10. Batten, D (1985), The New Division of Labor: the mobility of new technology and its impact on work, *Computers and Social Science 1*, 133-139.
11. Bagrit, L (1965), *The Age of Automation* (The Reith Lectures), Weidenfeld and Nicholson, London.
12. Smith, D J and Sage, M (1983), Computer Literacy and the Education/ Training Interface, *Computer Education 7*, 4 227-234.
13. Mabogunje, A L (1977), International Circumstances Affecting the Development and Trade of Developing Countries, in Ohlin, B, Hesselborn, P and Wijkman, P (eds), *The International Allocation of Economic Activity*, Macmillan, London, pp432-447.
14. Innis, H A (1951), *The Bias of Communication*, University of Toronto Press, Toronto (cited by Bell, D, op cit).

4. Computer communications — will they enable, or will they isolate?

Kate Bainbridge, *Transnet*
Kerry Hamilton, *Transnet*
Katy Oliver, *London Strategic Policy Unit*
Jane Smith, *Social and Community Planning Research*

This paper looks at some of the possible changes that may come about by computer communications through Wide Area Networks (WAN). It makes a comparison of the long-term effects that private transport (the motor car) has had on personal mobility with a similar situation in personal computer communications and suggests that many unacknowledged inequities and difficulties lie ahead.

New developments of any kind result in benefits for some and problems for others. Often, the magnitude of these benefits and problems are inter-related. For example, the myth that 'everyone has a car these days' is used to justify running down bus services for those who do not have access to a car.

It is unlikely that computer communications will be any exception to this 'two-edged' effect. Those who subscribe to these systems or are given access to them by the State will benefit, while those who somehow miss out will be even more isolated 'because everyone keeps in touch through the network these days' and the world will adapt surprisingly quickly to the demands and effects of such a system to the further detriment of those missing out.

Private transport
The acknowledged effects of having access to a car are generally positive:

— they take you where you want to go, when you want to go there

— they carry children, friends and shopping, in any combination, quickly and easily.

Other effects are not quite so positive:

— In 1986, in the United Kingdom 5,500 people were killed, 70,000 seriously injured and 320,000 hurt in traffic accidents (ROSPA figures — not yet finalised).

— The budget for maintaining this system is a) colossal, and b) impossible to assess accurately because it extends to road building, environmental deterioration, accident injuries, etc.

Even today, many people do not have access to a car and are never likely to. Statistics usually refer to 'households' rather than people and are often misleading because they do not show how few people have access to a car. These people include the elderly, those with low incomes, those whose partner uses the car during the day, children and those with disabilities.

This would not necessarily present a major problem, except that the car also has a wider effect on society. Land use patterns change in order to accommodate it. Drive-in services, super-stores for bulk buying, suburbs without corner shops or regular bus services, four-lane through-ways in city centres; many of them eyesores and few of them accessible by the walking public, who may be provided with a shopping precinct as some sort of alternative but very often no way to reach it except by car. These land use patterns do not encourage use of public transport, giving the operators a further chance to cut back services.

The entire economy is now structured to accommodate the primacy of private transport. The power of the 'road lobby', which includes the construction industry and the car industry, the oil industry and the road haulage industry, is proverbial; and all at the expense of the physical environment and certainly to the disadvantage of the majority of people who do not have access to private transport.

Economic structures have developed to mitigate the appalling loss of life and well-being caused by the motor car. For example, motor insurance is now a multi-million pound industry which permeates — often by statute — all aspects of our lives and deaths; and the National Health Service allocates a vast proportion of its limited resources on treating the results of this explosion of vehicles.

How has this state of affairs come about? The answer seems to be that those who make decisions already belong to the car-owning group, so they need not see or experience the negative aspects of their decisions, and status, prestige, fashion and commercial interests combine to make sure such trends continue. The result is a widening gap between those with and those without personal private transport.

Computer communications
It is not our intention to deny the undoubted advantages of computers, conferencing systems and wide area networks, particularly for the disabled and those living in remote areas. However, we do not yet know what will be the effect of doing all our shopping from home via keyboard and screen (for example). We would like to present here some more *potential* disadvantages.

— Computers enable you to communicate without face-to-face contact; no social skills are necessary

— PC chatter on the computer bulletin boards is still largely *about* chatter (like ham radio)

— The direct sensory experience of writing is lost and handwriting skills deteriorate

— PCs can be used to shut out the world

— Negative health effects are being registered

— Users can be hooked on games or on chatter to the exclusion of the real world or the family.

Two further illustrations
The implications of the way in which computer networks can be organised may be illustrated by reference to the generation and supply of electricity.

Although we would never deny the undoubted benefits arising from electricity, we do call into question the policy of relying on large centralised sources of power generation. This approach to the supply of power is not necessarily the most efficient or the most equitable. It certainly may not be the best for our physical environment.

Similarly with computers; we have seen what happened to the *organisation* of data processing when facilities were concentrated into the hands of a powerful few. It was not until computers became truly *personal* that applications began to appear that benefitted the ordinary person. When planning any future network for education we believe that a 'distributed' model is more likely to provide the best service for the user.

Conclusion
As professionals in social policy, we find ourselves constantly having to deal with the results of the iniquitous and unfair mess we have described above in relation to transport, a state of affairs which society now accepts.

We ask you to consider carefully the possible disadvantages that could arise from uncontrolled 'progress' and an uncritical enthusiasm for computer communications.

The question we wish to put to you is, how can you as professionals avoid similar future problems?

PART II

Electronic Communications and Practitioner Research

Teachers tend to spend much of their time in isolation from their colleagues and this isolation can be intellectual as well as physical. It is notoriously difficult for teachers to find out about developments in practice even within a neighbourhood, let alone in a national context. This is particularly true where classroom-based practitioner inquiry is concerned. Electronic communications media offer various ways of breaking out of this isolation, and the contributions in this section look into various ways in which the technology can be used to help teachers to share both the information and the process of making sense of it.

5. Information Technology and teacher-based action research (1)

Gordon Bell
Sheffield City Polytechnic
(now Professor of Education, Trent Polytechnic)

Part of this paper is based on a discussion document originally written in 1982.

Introduction
This contribution tries to explore some implications for the development of teacher based action research of recent advances in automated information retrieval and storage systems.

I have not attempted to present a fully developed argument but rather to put forward a case which focuses upon selected issues which arise from three main questions:

1. How are teachers to share their knowledge of practice?
2. How are teachers to collaborate effectively as researchers?
3. How are networks of teacher researchers to operate successfully?

I have tackled some aspects of these questions by assuming that the sharing of practical knowledge is largely a problem of disseminating teacher based action research, that effective collaboration amongst teacher researchers is largely a matter of how action research activities are to be co-ordinated, and that both of these approaches can be supported by the uses to which computerised information retrieval and storage systems may be put.

Some uses of computers to support action research projects
There are three main contexts within which teacher based action research can arise:

individual research, where a teacher works on a topic of investigation in isolation

collaborative research, where a group of teachers arrange to pursue some themes of inquiry in agreed form

network research, where groups or several individual teacher researchers agree to disseminate findings and exchange experience through some principle of multi-lateral co-operation (networking).

The latter two types, collaborative and network action research, require co-ordination. This raises questions as to the criteria which govern the direction of co-ordination.

The idea of a computerised database, particularly of the collaborative type, may be viewed as a form of neutral co-ordination. The participants voluntarily contribute records of where their research is presently going and other participants access the cumulative resources contained in the resultant database. In this way, an overview of the project can be independently arrived at by any participant.

The type of support gained by this method centres on using computers to provide information. However, computers may also be used to analyse and process the data generated by individual teacher researchers or groups.

Thus, two main applications of computers in teacher research can be identified:

a) computers as information retrieval and storage systems;

b) computers as data processing systems to analyse, sort and re-order data items.

Using computers as data handling devices becomes progressively more cost effective (as against manual methods), according to the volume of data, the degree of processing required to make sense of it, and the extent to which there is to be access to the information generated by the types of research undertaken.

Some implications of using computers to support action research projects

It would seem that there are different implications of using computers in various types of teacher research. For example, in my experience individual teacher research approaches a critical phase when a certain point of data collection has been passed; namely when manual methods of reviewing, analysing, re-ordering and preparing the evidence for report becomes more and more time consuming and less and less effective. At this point, any processing task generates further data which has, in turn, to be recorded, stored and retrieved. This process threatens to become overwhelming, either through the density of data, or through the amount of preparation needed for coherent reporting far exceeding the time available. In this connection, a computerised database can ease the problems of information flow for the individual teacher researcher, either by preventing overload (too many data items and too little time) and/or through a reduction in interim reporting required.

In collaborative and network teacher research, there is the added complication of co-ordinating information. This usually takes the form of letting other participants know what is 'going on' (diffusion of ideas). A database system can act as a means of reporting to individuals in such contexts, for it would be open to any participant to receive the complete listing of all records held on the database at any one time.

For co-ordinators and participants alike, there is an open system of monitoring implied in being able to see how any individual or group of individuals is functioning. This may be particularly useful in situations where individuals or groups are widely dispersed. Additionally, there is the further problem in all types of teacher research of making the outcomes known to non-participants. This raises questions about the form of reporting, the audiences which may be expected to receive the findings of action research, and the medium through which this is to be achieved. Such issues are classic symptoms of dissemination problems. A computerised database can be viewed as one method of dealing with certain of these demands.

Perhaps it is worth recalling at this point that project management issues have tended in the past to be described in terms of individual teachers providing data for a remote research team to process. In contrast, recent action research projects require teachers as novitiate researchers to process, prepare and analyse data and, incidentally, train themselves in appropriate techniques. The further complications of individual, collaborative and network research, to be managed at a distance on principles which satisfy the conditions of 'research' (as distinct from 'information' or 'finding out'), are highly complex, little discussed and central to the establishment of teacher research as a mode of inquiry. In advance of further discussion of these issues, a database system in collaborative research can act both as a means of report, a means of audit and a means of providing distance training.

In network research, all the foregoing elements of data preparation, processing and analysis, dissemination, report and co-ordination are present with the additional requirement that procedures for multi-lateral co-operation are identified. Moreover, in network research involving national networks of teacher researchers, issues of project management have close connections with what it is to establish a tradition of educational inquiry. In this regard, it is my contention that just as in the development of case study methodology where the distinction between case records and case study was proposed as fundamental, in action research a distinction between the *database* and the *report* is proposed as crucially significant.

I would therefore argue that:

1. *In the establishment of educational action research in general, and for the management of commissioned action research in particular, the notion of a database is conceptually necessary.*

2. *In the absence of forms of communication appropriate to the dissemination of practitioner research in general, and for the support of teacher research in particular, the setting up of an action research database is practically necessary.*

These assertions I hold to be central to the developing concept of teacher based action research. For it is one thing to talk about 'teacher research', quite another to secure those conditions that establish the findings of teacher based research as practical or educational *knowledge*.

Furthermore, if educational action research is logically distinct from more traditional conceptions of educational research (and this argument remains to be shown), then one might anticipate a distinctive mode of reporting to develop quite independent of current modes of scholarly communication.

Moreover, if one argues that teacher research is independent of existing educational knowledge and that such knowledge as is gained arises by means of different methods of inquiry, is there not a danger of continuous 're-invention of the wheel'?

However, if one admits that an existing body of knowledge developed by non-action research methods is relevant, what might be the criteria of relevance here? How, and at what points, may such knowledge be validly incorporated within an action research methodology?

Purposes and types of databases in teacher research
Such issues as these are crucial in the design of systems for recording and reporting professional practice. Decisions taken on these matters will have quite different practical effects. This may be illustrated with reference to the various purposes to which databases might be put and to the various types of databases that might be distinguished, for example:

PURPOSE OF DATABASE

Purpose A — to help teacher researchers to improve their method of researching so as to become more effective researchers;

and/or

Purpose B — to help teacher researchers to analyse their data more effectively;

and/or

Purpose C — to help process the data collected more easily, individually or in groups.

TYPES OF DATABASE

(a) a database used on an individual and independent basis;

(b) a database to be used as a means of co-ordinating collaborative research, whether in groups or in networks;

(c) a database containing the outcomes of recent and current research in progress, limited to action research projects only;

(d) a database containing the outcomes of recent and current teacher research, interpreted as any research project a teacher undertakes;

(e) a database with a record format restricted to bibliographic data;

(f) a database with a record format designed to accommodate any form of report;

(g) a database with conditions of access designed to reflect assumptions about what counts as educational/pedagogical/practical knowledge;

(h) a database which is interactive, and on-line, meaning that any teacher can at any time access the data and edit, retrieve or delete any or all of the records held;

(i) a database which is off-line, meaning that some intermediary updates and retrieves the data on request;

(j) a database which is refereed, implying that any data prepared for inclusion is reviewed in the light of some external set of criteria;

(k) a database which is limited in scope to that which might be housed on a microcomputer and located with the teacher researcher;

(l) a database which is limited in terms of the number of users it can support concurrently;

(m) a database which is limited in terms of the storage capacity made available on a mini or mainframe computer in some remote location.

Practical but tentative examples of various types of database which combine different purposes may be described as follows.

1. A mainframe, on or off-line, action research database: designed as an information retrieval and storage system (IR+S) to support individual collaborative and network research in the context of a specific commissioned project.

2. A mainframe, off-line, refereed, action research database: designed as an IR+S system to represent the current stage of development of action research in educational settings in a national context.

3.   A microcomputer based interactive database: designed as both an IR+S system and a data processing system to support individual or collaborative research in a specific context.

4.   A micro or mainframe based system combining one or more features of the above (1-3) and designed to support teacher based research in general.

(*Note*: 'On-line' means being able to have direct access to the stored information by using a telephone line and terminal. 'Off-line' means that a telephone call or postal request would be necessary to make any query, with the answer coming back at a later stage.)

These main models of the ways in which Information Technology might assist the development of teacher research are not meant to be mutually exclusive, nor are they exhaustive. They are not presented in any order of priority, nor are they the only possible models. They are, however, outlined as a way of pointing up various distinctions that might be drawn which may have an important bearing on the future development of teacher based research.

An outline of assumptions on the relevance of computers to teacher based action research

Let me now try to make explicit what practical matters might be implied in the provision of computerised databases in teacher research.

Individual teachers would find it very difficult to achieve those standards implicit in tasks of 'research' without access to data storage, retrieval and processing resources. These difficulties are multiplied when research is conducted without secretarial assistance or when the teacher concerned is not attached to some concurrent in-service course. Conducting collaborative research in the absence of some developed data preparation and processing system much impairs the functioning of this form of teacher research.

In conducting network research, and for as long as conditions obtain whereby what is reported by teacher participants cannot be systematically distributed in a form which bears cumulative and critical comparison, there can (logically) be no possibility of 'research' in the fullest sense of that term. No alternative tradition of inquiry will be developed. The attempt to co-operate will be grounded in social and political considerations at the expense of critical thinking about what counts as *knowledge* of practice.

What counts as a 'network' and, more importantly, how networks of teacher researchers actually achieve effective forms of multi-lateral co-operation, is an important question in this form of research. One definition of a 'network of teacher researchers' may be understood on an analogy with a collaborative database; the members of a network supply the information which all members agree to be most valuable to provide.

In this way, the value of disseminating outcomes, namely that they are of some use, is satisfied. Moreover, the kind of satisfaction presupposed is *structural* — ie the resources committed to disseminating information to particular groups are limited by the condition that a matching contribution is required. This 'bring and buy', or collaborative, principle is a necessary condition to the notion of co-operation which, in turn, is a pre-condition to making networks work in practice as distinct from theory.

Such an approach can be contrasted with the 'clearing house' principle, where suppliers of information have their information processed by third parties. In this situation, the community of users is controlled by inter-mediaries, who typically act as functionaries as distinct from participants. They are placed in positions of judgement as to when and who gets the information supplied. What counts as a network, in this instance, depends upon reactive mediation as distinct from interactive participation.

Both are 'responsive' in different yet arguably complementary ways. The strengths of the one are the weaknesses of the other. What I am asserting here is that teacher research will not be properly supported without provision for both; ie, access to a 'clearing house' and access to collaborative databases. A central assumption of this assertion is that one or several computerised databases will help teacher researchers to become more effective. The arguments which involve this assumption may be summarised in the following way.

One of the major difficulties for teachers researching their practice is finding time to do it. Another is getting started. The former is mainly a problem of research management; time to prepare, process and analyse data. The latter is a research training problem, involving access to various kinds of resources at different stages of 'getting started'.

In order to satisfy each of these conditions for effective teacher research, a third difficulty arises as to what counts as 'educational research' as distinct from 'systematically finding out' about something. If teacher research is to count as 'research' in the fullest sense that professional knowledge of educational practice is claimed, then other, much more problematic, criteria must be met.

Therefore, to improve the effectiveness of teachers researching their own practice:

(i)   research training issues need to be identified;

(ii) research project management issues need to be negotiated;

(iii) research dissemination issues need to be clarified.

All of this presupposes being clear about the conditions under which an alternative tradition of inquiry is developed and distinguished from existing conventions of educational research.

Such a tradition, it is argued, would typically centre upon practical questions arising in professional situations and rely upon systematic descriptions provided by practitioners in such contexts. The evidence generated in this way would be subject to critical appraisal, to verification by various tests, and be validated in dialogue with other competent judges.

A determining feature of attempts to make such research more effective is related to the question as to how sponsorship of this type of research is to be accomplished by appropriate forms of practical support. It is the focal theme of this discussion to suppose that computerised databases can make a contribution to this basic consideration.

A further and concluding consideration is that diffusion of information to participants in a teacher research project and dissemination of its outcomes to non-participants are necessary conditions to talk of research and to collaborative forms of action research in particular.

The adoption of a database definition of issues of dissemination and diffusion opens up an alternative approach to familiar difficulties concerned with how projects are to be evaluated, how they are to be co-ordinated, and how their outcomes are to be of use to others.

Computerised databases can be deployed in two main ways in relation to these matters. First, a collaborative database can be a ready means of monitoring the activities of large numbers of individual teacher researchers. Secondly, a database may be described as the product of a commissioned project. This would then become an alternative to the more usual criterion of the productivity of a project, ie the package of teaching materials which results from it. In the current climate of resourcing, such an approach may be distinctly preferable on financial grounds alone.

Coincidentally, some project outcomes imply a residue in the form of a project archive. Whilst this might satisfy the research criterion of public availability of evidence, there is the practically significant constraint of access to consider. However, a database relates the criterion of public availability to that of access, so meeting a difficulty implicit in the notion of a project archive.

Thus, two models of the use of computers to disseminate information emerge. Both depend upon the establishment of computerised databases. One type would be 'collaborative', where the users of data would also be the suppliers of data. This would not, however, rule out the possibility of non-participants gaining access to the information it contained. The remaining type would be mainly useful for supporting collaborative research between networks of teacher researchers. This 'independent' database would rely upon contributions of data from a much wider range of sources than simply the participants in any particular project.

In summary, a collaborative database would serve the interests of diffusion to participants in a specific project; an independent database might best serve the interests of dissemination in a wider sense.

Some provisional suggestions

Overall, taking into account the current state of teacher research, the demands inherent in establishing an alternative mode of inquiry, and what it is to sponsor and then to support modes of multi-lateral co-operation, I propose that action research databases are justified on the grounds that minimally:

1. They will promote the flow of information between individuals in a network of teacher researchers.

2. They will promote the flow of information between a network and external agencies.

3. They will satisfy some of the conditions necessary to talk of 'research'.

4. They will be a practical means of mediating the relating between an archive and its users.

5. They will be a means of promoting the flow of information between users and suppliers of data in action-research networks.

6. They will stimulate developments in other educational applications and settings.

7. They will provide an in-built staff development function in relation to Information Technology.

8. They will introduce procedures to which other information services can relate and from which other forms of data may be developed.

9. They will make teacher research more effective in providing research training, research management resources and research dissemination opportunities.

Postscript

Since the original working paper first appeared from which this contribution is derived, I have pursued certain of these suggestions to a further stage of development. This has involved four main initiatives:

i)   A small-scale survey of teacher researchers to identify which factors are considered most important to include in a database system to support teacher based action research.

ii)   An intensive study visit to investigate a computerised educational research information system designed on networking principles.

iii) A single site field trial of an interactive database developed in the context of a whole school practitioner research project using both remote mainframe and school based microcomputers.

iv)   A multi-site evaluation of a microcomputer program for information retrieval and storage to support teacher based action research.

In the first of these activities, teacher researchers in the inner and outer networks of the 'Teacher Pupil Interaction and Quality of Learning Project' identified thirty-five factors relevant to the design of database systems using the following question as a starting point for group discussion of the issues raised:

> 'What kind of information would best support your research at this stage and what kind of information do you envisage being most useful to you in the future?'

A composite list of factors compiled from the various discussion groups was then circulated to individual teacher researchers in the project and to other teacher researchers not connected directly with this project, for ranking of the items. Forty-three teachers responded and a profile of a possible database system can be described from their rankings.

Drawing upon this evidence, it would appear that top priority should be directed to including material which would assist in dealing with individual teachers' analysis of their own data. A second priority, which perhaps reflects the interests of teacher researchers in the TIQL project, concerns information on 'Teacher language and pupil language and its relevance to teaching for understanding'. Help with utilising existing knowledge came a very close third priority as expressed in the statement 'Existing examples of published research on the area chosen by the teacher'. A further qualification of the same theme was identified as 'Abstracts of teacher research from dissertations and short studies, not necessarily action research based'. More general concerns emerged in the fifth priority, namely 'Information on research about motivation and learning, particularly interest as opposed to examinations'.

The remaining two priorities to some extent overlapped with previous items and stressed the need for 'Up to date factual information, opinions, ideas, about the area chosen by the teacher' and information on 'Unpublished/ on-going classroom action research (and for example name, place, title including focus of study, age of pupils, duration, etc)'.

Passing now to the second of these follow-up activities, an intensive study visit was carried out in order to make detailed observations of a computerised system which has recently been developed at the Ministry of Education, Toronto, Ontario, Canada (2). Entitled ONTERIS (Ontario Educational Research Information System), its distinctive features are that it was designed to reflect the information requirements of administrators, teachers and professional researchers and to modify some perceived weaknesses of the major computerised system currently available, namely ERIC (Educational Resources Information Centre). In addition, the ONTERIS team saw the benefit of combining computerised systems in networks so as to maximise the transfer of information from one node in a system to that of another.

Several of these features seemed to be consonant with emerging issues in the design of a possible system for teacher researchers and to a considerable extent this was borne out in the subsequent visit, though I shall only have space here to highlight three such issues.

Firstly, the development principles used by the ONTERIS design team attempted to strike a balance between administrative, teaching and profes- sional research interests. A test of the adequacy of the solution reached is evident in the formats of records used as the main vehicle for the eventual system. These were developed as a means of structuring the information available and are a key consideration in the design of any database system. A related issue is the problem of identifying the types of educational information thought to be useful for various groups of users. (The ONTERIS feasibility study identified thirteen different types.)

Secondly, the ONTERIS system has evolved in the form of a suite of databases and not just one. Each has its own record format and distinctive focus. There are three main databases currently available to serve the interests of the educational community in the Province: CURR which is a database of 3,300 records (April 1982) of Ministry of Education Guidelines and support documents, and material from School Boards throughout the Province; EDUC a database of over 2,200 records of educational research documents from various agencies within the Province; ARCH a database containing archival records of material relating to Commissions, Reviews and Special Projects funded by the Ministry.

As an indication of the type of information available and of the structure of the record formats developed, I shall take the Curriculum Database Record (CURR) as an example. This database contains fifteen fields and includes a unique identifying number for each document; description of the type of document, eg guideline, handbook, bibliography resource, etc; whether the material is current or superseded; the language of the document; personal or corporate author; the responsible agency; title; place of publication; number of pages; curriculum subject area; age range; target population aimed at by the authors of the document; an abstract of contents; and notes to assist in identifying related records.

Thirdly, this example raises a further issue. This is the question as to how abstracting is to be handled in establishing a database system. Clearly, not all items of information can be included and some criteria of selection will be necessary. The ONTERIS team employed a distinction between the 'indicative' abstract and the 'informative' abstract. In the indicative type, no attempt is made to be a complete representation of the source material though the abstract provided must be a reliable guide to its form and content. This kind of abstract is used for those reports which contain so much information as to defy adequate summarisation. By way of contrast, the 'informative' abstract directly transmits the principal ideas, methods and data contained in the document to the reader and attempts to stand in place of the document itself.

A set of procedures for abstracting to these standards has been developed containing many useful pointers to overcoming the difficulties of rendering educational information in a form which can usefully be transferred to others. The aim is to avoid continuous re-reading of the same material, or searching the same body of literature, and generally to facilitate the development of practical knowledge, especially in networks of participants.

These twin themes of the cumulation of practical knowledge and increasing the flow of information between one teacher researcher and another, which are implications of a system like ONTERIS, may be viewed as one way of meeting a main criticism of teacher based research, a criticism that emanates from teacher researchers themselves. This is, of course, the perceived problem of generalising from the situation of one teacher researcher to that of another.

I cannot here enter into the philosophical questions this issue raises, except to suggest that the meaning of 'educational research' is the uses to which it is put. This implies that a future agenda for both teacher researcher use of other teacher researchers' work and teacher researchers' use of alternative modes of educational research lies in processes of verification and validation of existing knowledge in practice.

Selected aspects of these main concerns underpin the remaining activities I shall now briefly describe by way of illustrating some means by which the resources represented by new Information Technology might be harnessed in the development of teacher based research.

In one small-scale project, the aim is to see how well a microcomputer program originally designed to facilitate information retrieval and storage in schools can be adapted for use in the context of teacher based action research. An evaluation of the impact of microcomputer based systems on the processes of such research will be a secondary aim (3).

In the second project, many of the underlying principles I have attempted to raise in this review are being field tested in a whole school practitioner research context (4). The project has three main features. Firstly, it relies upon the notion of 'practitioner research' meaning that it includes participants other than teachers. This is particularly relevant in relation to the issue which provides the focus of the project, ie the school's policy in relation to the integration of children with special educational needs into mainstream (primary) classes. Secondly, it uses the term 'action inquiry' to denote a particular methodology that requires a strategic relationship between case study techniques and action research methods. Thirdly, the project relies on establishing appropriate databases to support the processes of conducting this form of school based research, especially those processes concerned with the utilisation of existing knowledge and the transfer of knowledge between participants and other interested practitioners.

The project team addressed the problem of agreeing protocols in the form or record formats to structure the transfer of knowledge being gained in the processes of data collection and data analysis by individuals and sub-groups. These protocols may be expected to reflect the interests of practitioners other than teachers and will need to accommodate data from both case and action research and include information from a body of existing literature.

Conclusion

There are signs of quickening interest in the opportunities afforded by new Information Technology in supporting teacher based research. In this contribution, I have attempted to identify some issues relevant to this effort and describe some initiatives taken to make practical headway in this direction.

The main constraints currently appear to be suitable software for the wide variety of hardware available; prejudices about computers; difficulties in liaison between established and newly developed disciplines — particularly computer scientists, librarians, teacher researchers, advisers and other consultants; too few field based projects which bring existing agencies together — especially advisers, teacher trainers, parents, headteachers and teachers; relative ignorance about the concepts of networks and networking in the context of practitioner research; and unsystematic attention paid to the utilisation of existing knowledge in the process of educational decision making.

What is needed is greater collaboration between existing agencies, direct funding of short-term, small-scale efforts at the school level, perhaps in the manner pioneered by Schools Council, Programme Two, and better understanding of the processes of developing and using practical professional knowledge.

Notes and references
1.   This contribution is a version of Part Two of a fuller report, *Electronic Action Research Networks: Progress Report of a Feasibility Study,* submitted by the author to the Schools Council, Programme Two in March 1982 and which also appeared in edited form as Working Paper 9 of the Teacher Pupil Interaction and Quality of Learning Project under the title Information Technology and Teacher Research: A Discussion Paper Sale, Ebbutt, D and Elliott, J (1985), *Issues in Teaching for Understanding,* Longman, ch 1.
2.   Bell, G H (1983), Computerised Educational Research Information in Ontario, Canada: A Case Report of a Study Visit, *Collected Original Resources in Education,* Vol 7, No 1.
3.   Bell, G H (1985), SIR and Teacher Based Research: A Pilot Evaluation, British Library Research and Development Department Report 5829, *Collected Original Resources in Education,* Vol 9, No 1.
4.   Bell, G H and Colbeck, B (1984), Whole School Practitioner Research: The Sunnyside Action Inquiry Project, *Educational Research,* Vol 26, No 2.

6. Electronic communications media and networking in practitioner research

David Smith
Centre for Evaluation of Information Technology in Education (CITE); National Foundation for Educational Research

This article is based on a Briefing Report given to a seminar entitled 'Practitioner research: the role of networks and networking', Thornbridge Hall, Bakewell, Derbyshire, June 1987. The seminar was organised by Sheffield Polytechnic Department of Education and sponsored by the British Educational Research Association (BERA).

Introduction

Education is constantly inflicted with solutions in search of problems and, before making specific proposals, we need to be reasonably sure what we are trying to achieve. We must avoid being driven by technology rather than by human needs but, at the same time, we need to avoid technophobic luddism. Certain things are possible with new IT which are not possible in any other way. In this respect, computer-based communications systems may offer advantages (and disadvantages!) which cannot be predicted on the basis of experience with conventional systems. The role of advanced communications systems is a burgeoning research field in its own right. What we can discuss here are not ready-made off-the-peg solutions to clearly articulated problems but rather avenues for further research and development, some possibilities for which will be explored in the specific context of this paper.

In examining networking, we are dealing with a broad spectrum of communication needs, some requiring high speed operation and a high level of interactivity, others needing only slow communications and a relatively low level of interactivity. The information which we are communicating has a wide range of 'half-life', from 'tablets of stone' permanence to light-hearted triviality. Our needs are complex and are matched by an equally complex technical 'batterie de cuisine'. 'Information Technology' is not just a term to help us avoid using the word 'computer' too often in one paragraph! It covers a whole range of technologies, some of which are well established and many of which are still relatively undeveloped. These technologies offer a wide range of potential channels for the communication of professional information at all levels in the educational system. Broadcast television, cable narrowcasting, teletext, viewdata, electronic mail systems, computer databases and many others may all have important, if specialised, roles to play.

Context

There is widespread (but by no means universal) agreement about the potential importance of practitioner research networks in education and it is not my purpose here to attempt to establish a case for them! What I want to do, however, is to try to identify some aspects of such networks which may be either enhanced or even actually enabled by the use of modern electronics communications media.

Comparison between the two human-centred disciplines of medicine and education may be helpful here. The sort of cumulative body of professional case knowledge which partly underpins the coherence of the medical profession requires close attention to communication. The medical profession has evolved channels of communication and frameworks for description whereby the direct experience of the individual practitioner may be shared with others and incorporated into a larger corpus of professional 'wisdom'. Education, by contrast, has been rather slow in giving attention to the dynamics of information flow.

Part of the function of a network is to develop a professional climate in which data and ideas are shared as widely and as effectively as possible. It is very easy, however, to invent grand global strategies which take no account of human intentions and we need to keep our ideas firmly rooted in the real world. Practitioners undertake research for a whole variety of reasons — often in relation to purely temporary and/or local needs. They are not necessarily fired by missionary zeal or by a burning desire to contribute to a 'corpus of professional wisdom'! Many people wish to keep control over their own ideas and they ought to retain that right. All the same, what is in many respects a purely personal or local matter could also be the missing piece from someone else's jigsaw.

It is ironic that the 'learned journals' arose in response to just these issues, by making public channels of communication which were previously restricted to 'hidden colleges' of workers who shared ideas face-to-face or by correspondence. But journals rapidly become pillars of orthodoxy, shutting out mere teachers. Even practitioner newsletters have a disconcerting habit of going up-market and joining the academic Brownie-point system, adding both to the endless proliferation of journals and to the pressure on practitioners who wish to keep up with developments. And the lethargic pace of publication limits the value of what is on offer. For example, articles in the March 1987 edition of the *Journal of Computer Assisted Learning* were accepted for publication in or before March 1986. Please note that this is cited as a typical case — *JCAL* is not particularly bad in this respect.

Accessibility, ownership and speed may be critical factors in establishing the sort of professional climate we are discussing and this is where modern electronic communications systems may well come into their own.

Electronic systems and practitioner networks
It was suggested above that new Information Technologies offer a very wide range of channels for the communication of different kinds of information. However, three types of system seem especially suited to the communications needs of practitioner research networks:

a) Databases
A database is essentially a computerised filing system. There are various systems for the classification of information in databases and various ways of finding information. Some of the best-known public access databases are on British Telecom's Prestel system, and there are many others.

Many problems with databases are really clerical rather than technical. The systems do not run themselves, so somebody has to undertake the tasks of *data capture* (getting the information) and *data entry* (getting it into the computer). Once the system is up and running, potential users must be able to get at the information it contains. Finally, someone has to take on the *housekeeping* function, keeping the system up to date and checking the accuracy of information (even before we mention the Data Protection Act!!). Not impossible or even particularly difficult, but implying a layer of organisation which could interpose itself between participants and might impede the free operation of a network.

b) Electronic Mail
Electronic Mail (E-mail) systems offer high-speed communications between computer terminals. One computer, the *host*, runs the controlling software (in practice, the host may be a network of computers). Users connect their own computers with the host through a telephone link called a *modem*. Chunks of text *(messages)* may be written into a reserved file in the host computer. This file is called a *mailbox* (MBX!). Only an authorised person can read the contents of each mailbox but other systems users can send messages to it. Messages can be sent to a large number of mailboxes simultaneously and nearly instantaneously. Systems users can read their mailboxes or send messages at any time suitable to themselves. Messages can be *downloaded* and saved (for example on a disk) for later consideration, or they can be read directly. It is possible to check whether messages have been inspected by their intended recipients!

E-mail systems permit rapid and relatively cheap communication between network members. It is possible to exchange quite substantial documents, which can be prepared *off-line* on a suitable word-processing system. Thus, several persons can work collaboratively on documents. It is possible to set up a *bulletin board* into which messages can be written. The bulletin board can be 'closed', so that only group members can read it, or it can be open to the public.

The best-known E-mail system in education is TTNS (The Times Network Systems) but Prestel also supports E-mail and there are several other systems, including the commercial BT Gold and the research-based ESRCNET.

c) Electronic Conference Systems

Although computer conferencing is widely used in industry and commerce, it has so far found few educational applications in the UK (the Open University's CoSy is one exception). By contrast, there are numerous systems in use in countries such as the USA and Canada. Computer conferencing is based on E-mail but offers more complex messaging and group communication facilities. A good conference system allows the simultaneous progress of a number of 'conferences'. Each conference comprises a number of *items*. An individual may participate in a number of conferences at the same time and may even contribute the same item to different conferences (not unlike academics anywhere!).

Good conference systems offer facilities such as closed conferences, open conferences, bulletin boards, databases and simultaneous 'chat' lines. Current systems include CIX, PARTICIPATE, CAUCUS, CoSy and many others.

At the moment, most E-mail based systems have numerous defects. Current systems are not as 'user-friendly' as they might be (some are, on the contrary, almost 'user-savage'!) and this is likely to deter many potential users. In addition, indirect communication by computer misses many of the cues and signals which make direct face-to-face transactions meaningful (things like intonation, 'body language', etc). But, at the same time, the lack of direct contact may also be an advantage. Participants in a network are under no pressure to respond instantaneously to questions or ideas. The feeling of somehow being permanently under examination is simply not there when you can make your contribution at any convenient time. There is undoubtedly an element of stress in working with electronic communications but it is a new sort of stress. Whether that makes a difference is a research issue in itself! Where these systems, and particularly conferencing systems, *do* score heavily is in their potential for the liberation of practitioners from the loneliness and isolation which are often part and parcel of small-scale enquiry.

A workable system?
It is my opinion that some (certainly not all!) of the current problems of practitioner research networking could be solved by the use of a suitable computer-based conferencing environment. There are a number of systems which could provide the basic 'bones' of the network and I am not advocating any specific technical solution.

We at CITE have been thinking in terms of the 'Electronic Teachers' Centre' (which is the brainchild of my colleague Ros Keep). This is a way of conceptualising a quite complex conferencing system in terms of something we all know and love! The 'Centre' is described in detail in an earlier paper but basically would comprise:

a) 'Seminars': specific conferences which could be closed or open to outsiders but which would be announced so that 'visitors' would know what was going on at any one time;

b) 'Noticeboards': bulletin boards where interesting information could be displayed for a fixed period of time;

c) 'Coffee room': an open-access 'chat' system;

d) 'Print room': various publishing options — chiefly electronic, of course;

e) 'Library': an intelligent database system with extensive search facilities;

f) 'Switchboard': gateways into other systems;

g) 'Notepad': a personal note file.

We simply don't know how (or even whether) this would all work. But we regard it as a challenging research and development environment.

Using the 'Electronic Teachers' Centre' principle, teachers and other educators could take part in professional discussions over a long period of time, contributing to the development of ideas and the evolution of a language of discourse in their field; and they could do so without the need for frequent face-to-face meetings. The products and/or the processes of these discussions could be made accessible to a wide audience. Instead of producing a mosaic of unrelated and isolated facts, practitioner researchers should be able to contribute significantly to an ongoing process of professional development — in the sense of the development of the profession itself, as well as in the narrower personal sense. But this is *potential*. It is up to us to turn it into reality.

Some priorities
We clearly need to know a great deal more about the ways in which electronic systems may support (or even undermine!) the growth and

effectiveness of practitioner networks. I am not proposing a detailed research programme here but our research priorities might include:

a)   The evolution of a specific language of discourse mediated by electronic communications systems;

b)   'Knowledge Transfer' problems related to the elicitation of professional knowledge at the propositional and deep knowledge levels;

c)   The social dynamics of electronically mediated interaction;

d)   The effectiveness of electronic networks in supporting local curriculum developments;

e)   The growth of an 'electronic grey literature'.

There are many other issues here and I do not simply want to write a catalogue of them. But one point stands out above all. The whole thing will require relatively high levels of financial and human resourcing. Very little can be achieved on the basis of piecemeal local efforts. Nor should we be forced to be the captive clients of commercial systems. We have a higher purpose than merely to provide lucrative markets for organisations whose interest in education may be temporary and superficial. At its root, this is a matter for government intervention on a relatively large scale. Whether we will get it is quite another thing.

Bibliography

Publication on this topic is understandably somewhat thin on the ground! The following may be worth consulting:

Bacsich, P, Kaye, A and Lefrere, P (1986), An International Survey of Information Technologies for Education and Training, *Oxford Surveys in Information Technology 3*, pp 271-318.

Gaines, B and Shaw, M (1984), *The Art of Computer Conversation: a new medium for communication*, Prentice Hall, Englewood Cliffs.

Harasim, L and Johnson, M (1986), *Research on the Educational Applications of Computer Networks for Teachers and Trainers in Ontario*, Ontario Ministry of Education, Toronto.

Kaye, A (1987), Introducing Computer-mediated Communication into a Distance Education System, *Canadian Journal of Educational Communications 16*, 2.

Kaye, A (1987), On-line Services for Schools: an appraisal, in Jones, A and Scrimshaw, P (eds), *Computers in Education 5-13*, Open University Press.

Meeks, B N (1987), The Quiet Revolution, *BYTE*, February 1987, pp 184-197.

7. Mutual support systems

Tony Scott
University of Sussex and Croydon LEA

Good advisers are never in the office; good teachers are never out of the classroom. If life were really like that then the spread of good ideas and good practice across any but the smallest authorities would be an extremely slow process. Innovation does take place, ideas are exchanged and problems solved, through telephone conversations and face-to-face interactions in meetings, conferences, interviews. But, because of the tyranny of the timetable and the vagaries of the transport system, at a very great cost in money, time and stress.

Surveys of telephone use in commerce and industry put the chances of making contact directly with a required individual at no more than 30 per cent. Messages of any technical complexity or length are best not left to a secretary or an answering machine; letters are expensive to create (even when the secretary has a word processor) and slow to deliver. The financial sector has long realised that the oil of technology, and particularly • communications technology, is necessary to keep the wheels of commerce moving. How much more so then, in a situation where the advisers are in constant motion and the advisees constantly otherwise engaged.

Not that teachers only have an adviser/advisee relationship with their inspectors. They are also experts together in particular branches of the profession and share more common ground perhaps, as historians or home economists, than with their colleagues in schools or inspectorates.

Electronic mail provides opportunities to create services that recognise and overcome difficulties of communication within an authority and enhance communication between (individuals in) authorities.

Perhaps the most striking example of the power of electronic mail is its ability to provide detailed, technical support. Many Times Network Systems managers are grateful to Geoff Parkin of Hampshire (YMT001) for detailed help with the organisation of that system and the provision of, for example, computer programs to estimate telephone costs. Support which has been received without the need to travel to or from Hampshire or to be on the 'phone at any particular time. In the London Borough of Croydon, we are experimenting with a system which provides technical support for the management of computer systems, and especially computer networks, from a variety of sources. Individual teachers are designated 'consultants' in particular systems and enquiries are directed or re-directed to their box numbers. Responses are despatched to enquirers and filed centrally to become the basis of an on-line searchable problem/solution database. This approach has some of the characteristics of on-line help systems in the computer services industry but has the extra dimension of *diffused* expertise. Obviously, these teacher consultants formulate a network amongst themselves seeking help for more intractable problems or checking out suggested solutions. Attempts are being made to extend this network by incorporating the manufacturers as participants, but with little success to date.

As well as the other mutual support networks one can envisage within an authority (eg PE teachers arranging matches), one can envisage national networks of those with particular interests (eg SPORTNET). This may vary from 'formal' networks such as NAACE, where all computer advisers are provided with mailboxes, to informal national networks of, say, music teachers interested in the application of computers or the use of a particular synthesiser, or birdwatchers reporting sightings to each other of rare species. There is probably even a network somewhere of researchers into electronic mail networking.

One might view this range of networks in two categories: those which are expressions through electronic mail of formal organisations (NAACE), informal gatherings (NFER), or professional societies; and those which are perhaps more spontaneous or informal electronic gatherings.

There are three problems with the latter category — who creates them? How does their membership grow? How long are they self-sustaining? — on which the work of community psychologists and social analysts might shed some light.

Creating informal mutual support systems may well be the result of individual initiative by a facilitator (or 'animateur') perceiving or acting on a problem or an individual searching for help ('can anyone out there tell me about...?'), or of an organisational decision by an appropriate body, 'go out there and create a community spirit about...'

Three experiments we are embarked on that are related to users of TTNS may be of interest here: A Personal and Social Education Advisers' Network, an Esperanto Users' Network, and a Regional Adult Education Network.

Personal and Social Education is in many respects a 'new' curriculum area, although it is constituted of elements that have long been the hallmark of successful schooling. Croydon's Adviser for PSE has responsibility for INSET support for careers, health, outdoor pursuits and RE teachers, and for pastoral education and 'preparation for adult life' courses. Other PSE advisers have similar but never matching responsibilities. PSE advisers are trying to establish role definitions and an appropriate intellectual framework. They do not as yet have a clearly-identifiable national body or forum in which to exchange views, although their paths might cross at twenty different kinds of conference. We are taking an initiative, then, to see if we can establish an electronic mail network of PSE advisers; but a limited initiative, as approaches are being made through the network. We suspect more direct initiatives will be needed to get it off the ground. This, then, will be an initiative 'across authorities'.

The next experiment at creating a mutual support system will be both wider and narrower in scope. Wider in that it will attempt to be international, narrower in that it will be focused on developing participants' facilities in written Esperanto. This initiative will begin with a two-pronged appeal — through the network to identify current TTNS users who are also, or who may wish to become, Esperanto users, and presentations about TTNS and the possibilities of international electronic mail, to gatherings of Esperantists. It is hoped to establish a (mediated) social network between Esperantists and to develop tutor/learner relationships through the system.

The third experiment which is envisaged is to establish the use of electronic mail by a network of adult education co-ordinators in East and West Sussex, who currently meet together occasionally, to maintain contact between these meetings, to keep each other notified of vacancies on courses, of potential tutors and subjects for future courses. If successful, this network will bridge across adult, higher and further education institutions.

Once launched, the pattern of growth of these informal mutual support systems will vary according to the nature of the participants. The PSE Advisers' Network has a natural limit of about 104 education authorities — first enquiries were from the Isle of Wight, the Isle of Man and the Shetland Islands! Whether the network reaches its 'natural' limit depends not only on the benefit which potential participants may perceive in it but on the profile of TTNS amongst currently non-subscribing authorities.

The Esperanto network, if it becomes established, will have a considerable scope for future expansion, limited only by access to PSS and Dialcom services throughout the world, being embedded in a potential audience of eight million Esperanto users. (We believe a significant proportion of the one million fluent Esperanto speakers to be in education-related jobs.) It will be interesting to see if this social and mutual support network will be capable of extending beyond its initial education base.

The East/West Sussex Adult Education Network will have a double constraint of potential membership and geographical spread. The interest here will be in the links which it can form into local industry and commerce, and between the adult education network and various professional/subject networks.

It may be that social networks have a natural lifespan, particularly when they are related to an activity (eg a Jubilee street party) or a problem (an environmental protest). It may also be that once access to electronic networks is widespread, such spontaneous, focused groups will come into being through the network for the duration of a problem and then disperse. As things stand at the moment, however, one has to join such an initiative through a conscious act, become a subscriber, enrol on a computer which has the conference in which you are interested on it. This supports and tends to emphasise the formal aspects of networking. It may also be that this requirement for commitment tends to encourage the continuation of networks beyond a natural span. We need to do some comparative work on the larger and longer-established networks in the USA to find this out, perhaps as one of a series of cross-cultural studies of attitudes to using electronic media for social and problem-centred networking.

Certainly, there is a role for computer-mediated communication systems in promoting mutual aid between individuals, between individuals and organisations, and between organisations. The filtering out of cultural and status markers by electronic mail systems seems to be a significant factor in enabling and promoting co-operation across traditional boundaries.

It remains to be seen if they will provide a channel which enables geographically separated individuals to organise around enthusiasms.

8. Practitioner researchers and the microcomputer: a joint project between Sheffield University Division of Education and Sheffield City Polytechnic Department of Education

Susan Dennis
Teacher Fellow, Sheffield University, Division of Education

This report summarises a study of the potential use of microcomputers for information retrieval to support a network of practitioner researchers involved in action inquiry.

Practitioners have little or no access to knowledge of educational practice outside their locality and very little time to locate information for themselves. Such information frequently resides in university and polytechnic libraries that do not normally interact closely with the local school systems outside the framework of award bearing courses.

Action inquiry requires the use of existing knowledge and experience as teachers (and others) collect and analyse data in a cycle of research events, where the outcomes are to ground theory in practice and link practitioners to research. Closing the gap between the knowledge producers and potential users is where a microcomputer database can provide a link. This permits person to person contact, enabling ideas and expertise to be exchanged, disseminating knowledge and promoting interpersonal networks.

A small-scale survey of practitioner researchers' needs indicated that bibliographic information, local initiatives, reports, projects, resources and consultants were necessary elements of a microcomputer based system to support networking.

To accommodate this variety of information, several databases would ideally be needed to provide both 'servicing' and 'interactive' networks:

A servicing network would require a 'suite' of databases that included bibliographic and resource information provided by a volunteer reader group, the information being distributed to practitioners as a service.

An interactive network would require a 'suite' of databases that included action inquiries in progress and the outcomes of recent practitioner research, with contacts' names and localities being provided in each case. This suite of databases would provide a cost effective communication process, whereby the practitioner accesses existing knowledge and experience and through the same medium makes a contribution to its development.

For any database to have continued value, the information it contains must be regularly and frequently updated in order to maintain accuracy of data. The system studied involved the notion of 'disk swapping' where disks are returned to a central point to have the information updated.

Microcomputer databases used in the context of practitioner research not only provide for knowledge utilisation but can, with an additional service to provide relevant resources at a central point, essentially guarantee documentary retrieval success for the user. This removes one currently important source of blockage to practitioners.

Establishing a microcomputer based information retrieval and storage system along the lines proposed in the Feasibility Study would require further evaluation of its appropriateness as a means of support to practitioner researchers. A future investigation is planned to test its effectiveness in aiding decision making and to evaluate the strengths of the link between using practitioner research information and improving practice.

References

Dennis, S (1986), *Practitioner Researchers and the Microcomputer: A Feasibility Study*, Sheffield University/Sheffield City Polytechnic.

Dennis, S (1987), *Practitioner Researchers and the Microcomputer: A Pilot Network*, Sheffield City Polytechnic/British Educational Research Association Seminar, June (Mimeo).

Dennis, S (1987), *Collaborative Networking: An Evaluation of an Action Group*, Humberside LEA/Sheffield City Polytechnic (Mimeo).

PART III

Electronic Communications and Open Learning

The mushroom growth of 'open learning' is one of the success stories of recent years but there are many unanswered questions which have yet to be tackled. How, for example, do we provide tutorial support for students who may be working shifts and spread all over the country? Electronic communications media have obvious appeal here and the contributions which follow examine some of the implications of computer based media for open learning and, equally important, the implications of open learning for the new media.

PART II

Electronic Communication and Crew Reporting

9. Open learning systems: open learning technologies

Dick Davies
HIT Project, Southampton Institute

Two factors make this an opportune time to begin to attempt to conceptualise the relationship between open learning approaches and information technology:

— the current interest in open or flexible learning methods and resource based student centred teaching methods;

— the development of a range of applied information technologies in education.

This paper attempts to:

1. Depict the functions of the total educational process within an idealised open learning setting using a systems methodology.

2. Identify the information technologies that have a potential role within the components that constitute the process.

3. Mark those areas that use common technologies.

4. Prioritise research and development needs using an assessment of the ability of existing and emerging technologies to meet the needs of these sub-systems.

1. Open learning systems
Rather than trying to present an analysis in words, the diagram (Fig 9.1, page 68) attempts to depict educational sub-systems and their relationships. This does not imply any acceptance of the integrity of the system described, simply that systems theory provides a useful analytical tool (1) even when applied to ill-defined situations or so-called 'soft systems' (2).

2. Open learning technologies
Taking the systems diagram as a template, a further diagram (Fig 9.2, page 69) adds in information technology applications in an attempt to operationalise the identified sub-systems in terms of appropriate information technologies.

3. Key technologies for open learning systems
The exercise above pinpoints information technologies that are common to a number of sub-systems. Whilst more work is needed to flesh out the detail of each of these areas, it is possible at this early stage to list those

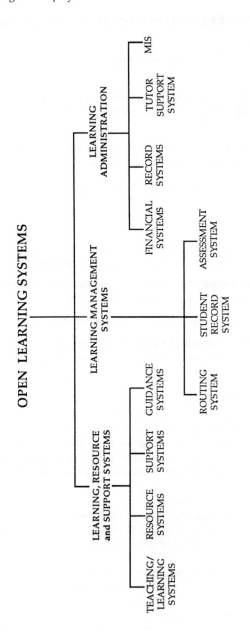

Fig 9.1 — Open learning systems

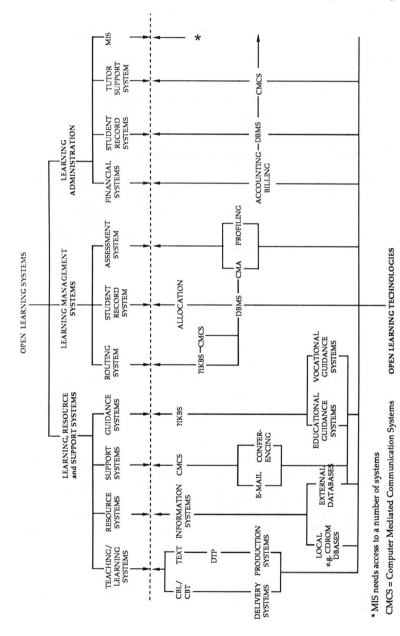

Fig 9.2 — Open learning technologies

* MIS needs access to a number of systems

CMCS = Computer Mediated Communication Systems

available technologies that have application outside individual sub-systems:

Standard applications software — text processors; spreadsheets; simple filing systems
Courseware production systems: authoring languages systems; desktop publishing systems
Computer mediated communication systems
Database management systems and information systems
Tailored administrative systems
Learning management systems.

4. Future needs for advanced open learning systems

Advanced open learning systems are those distance learning systems that are underpinned by information technologies. Distance delivery systems must rely on students having appropriate interfaces to these systems. In terms of technology, presumably these will centre on personal micro-computers and will require standard applications packages for text processing, number manipulation, file handling and, importantly, for communication to external data networks.

Key areas for development include:

a) Computer mediated communication systems
These systems, apart from offering messaging facilities, will also offer conferencing and access to 'electronic courses' (3).

Factors of key importance here include user interface to communications software and systems, network costs, systems costs, need to gateway between systems. Users need inexpensive local access to understanding human fault tolerant remote communication facilities. The other key area is work into the nature of the interaction that occurs in using these systems for teaching and learning (4).

b) Integrated administration systems for open learning
I offer no apology for making this unglamorous area a major priority. Any form of delivery system needs administrative support. Less time and cost in this area means more time on delivery and support. In terms of rapid payoff for both investors in and users of open learning systems, an efficient administration system, which after all only requires adaptation of existing applications packages, not new and expensive research, is simple to get up and running (5).

c) Support systems
As experience has shown, a major element in successful learning is adequate support systems. The role of computer mediated communications systems in this needs to be carefully evaluated (6).

d) Course and instructional design systems
The use of design methods based on software production techniques and knowledge engineering (7) (8). This would include knowledge elicitation and representation techniques and user interface design management systems.

e) Guidance systems
The automation of guidance (9) in learning systems, support systems and in course production systems is dependent on IKBS developments but is an important future element to be considered for mass delivery.

References
1. Von Bertalanffy, L (1962), General System Theory — A Critical Review, in *General Systems VII*, 1-20.
2. Checkland, P (1981), Systems Thinking. Systems Practice, in Shaw, M L and Gaines, B R (1986), *Interactive Elicitation of Knowledge from Experts 1*, 2 151-190.
3. Davie, L and Palmer (1984), Computer Teleconferencing for Advanced Distance Education, *Canadian Journal of University Continuing Education* X, 2 56-66.
4. Kerr, E B and Hiltz, S R (1982), *Computer Mediated Communication Systems: Status and Evaluation*, Academic Press, New York.
5. eg Use of MAIL and CAMELOT at National Extension College and CML systems at the Open University.
6. Hiltz, S (1985), *The Virtual Classroom: initial explorations of computer mediated communication systems as an interactive learning space*, NJIT, Newark.
7. Plamondon, R and Deschenes, J (1986), Course Design Using Software Engineering Methods, *Computer Education 10*, 4 417-427.
8. Rushby, N (1986), A Knowledge Engineering Approach to Instructional Design, *PLET 23*, 3 282-288.
9. Jackson, P and Lefrere, P (1984), On the Application of Rule-based Techniques to the Design of Advice-giving Systems, *International Journal of Man-Machine Studies 20*, 63-86.

10. Satellites — a life-line for open learning?

Judith Christian-Carter and Jane Burton
National Council for Educational Technology

Depending on who you talk to, you could be forgiven for thinking that satellites are going to be the answer to all the problems which currently beset open learning. Problems such as getting access to learning materials, the need to provide high quality materials, and the provision of two-way communication, both visual and audio, will be things of the past in the satellite era! Perhaps the 1990s version of Charles Dickens' 'Hot Mutton and Crumpet Company' will appear as the 'United Satellite Improved Educational and Training and Punctual Delivery Company'!

However, it would be an unwise person who would dismiss such claims as futuristic mumbo-jumbo and pie-in-the-sky thinking. The potential of any leading-edge information technology must be explored most carefully in order to ascertain any advantages that this new technology may have over more conventional methods. The claims of the 'satellite buffs' must be taken seriously and answers provided to the question, 'are satellites a life-line to open learning?', if we are not to overlook a potentially useful delivery mechanism.

What are satellites?
Essentially, satellites are transmitting and receiving devices situated in one of two orbits above the earth. Some satellites are in polar orbit of about 1,000 metres which means that each day they cover the whole globe from north to south, or vice versa, in a given number of passes. These low-orbiting satellites are mainly used for scanning the earth (land, sea and weather) and are used for remote sensing, ie observation of the earth from a distance via satellite. Other satellites are in geosynchronous orbit of about 36,000 metres which means that from earth they appear stationary in the sky. Some of these satellites are also used for remote sensing but, in the main, most of them act as both transmitting and receiving devices for communication and broadcasting purposes. Depending upon their power and location in the sky, their 'footprint' will cover a certain area constantly. The higher the transmitting power of the satellite, the larger the footprint.

What can satellites do?
There are four main educational uses of satellites: remote sensing; data transfer; broadcasting; and video conferencing.

Mention has already been made of remote sensing. Remote sensing is a quite different, as well as a very specific, use of certain types of satellite and, whilst it does have the potential to make a considerable educational contribution, it has no role to play in the delivery of open learning.

However, the uses to which data transfer, broadcasting and video conferencing can be put in open learning are potentially quite exciting and, as yet, generally under-explored. So what does each offer the open learner?

Data transfer
Data transfer is a use of satellites about which most of us are unaware. For example, when we dial the USA or Australia it matters little, provided the line is clear, how our voice is being transmitted, by terrestial land lines or by satellite. Access to computers in other parts of the world for the purposes of interrogating databases, sending and receiving electronic mail, and for computer conferencing may be achieved with or without satellite. Depending on the amount of traffic, the unseen controller sends your voice, instructions, or data automatically along one of the many routes available, and do you care or even want to know which route is being used?

But what if you were responsible on behalf of your international multi-million pound company for sending and receiving vital, and confidential, business data, such as share prices, bids, contracts, deals, profit and loss accounts, between the UK and the parent company in the USA? The cost of sending and receiving such information is not relevant but what is important is that the information must be sent and received as quickly and as reliably as possible by the most secure means possible. What do you do? Well, the answer is quite simple, you use a satellite link, engaging on the UK side the services of British Telecom International or Mercury.

Because the UK's educational and training system is not in the same financial league as business and commerce, and it is unlikely that it ever will be, data transfer has remained low on the list of potential uses of existing satellites. However, as discussed below, satellite technology is jumping ahead in great leaps and bounds in much the same way as people's thinking is developing on how to utilise these advances for learning. At the moment, the use of satellites for planned, deliberate and overt data transmission is out of the question but in another five to ten years it may be a completely different picture.

Broadcasting
Broadcasting is probably the thing which most people associate with satellites, the others being more fanciful notions of satellites being used for spying and for helping to 'zap' hostile missiles out of the sky. Because of satellites, we can watch 'live' the Olympic Games as they happen on the

other side of the world (that is if sleep hasn't caught up with us first!). The knowledge that a broadcast is coming to us 'live by satellite' probably means very little, in much the same way as data transmission does by this means. The broadcast channel we are watching is controlling and paying for the transmission. All we have done is to switch the television on, in just the same way as we would if we wanted to watch an Open College or Open University programme. We may even decide that, as the live satellite transmission is in the early hours of the morning, it would be more sensible to record it on videotape so we can watch it later at a more convenient time.

But what if you could receive a variety of satellite broadcasts, via different channels, all adding up to a wealth of different programmes from different countries? For some people, this wider provision of broadcasting entertainment has proved irresistible. For about 250,000 people (1% of all those who own television sets), cable TV is the means by which such variety is brought into their homes. Earth stations in the UK which receive satellite transmissions feed these into the cable network, allowing subscribers to watch a number of different broadcast channels. The more cable networks we have in the UK, the greater and wider this type of provision will be.

Satellite transmissions provided by cable are of a high quality. The earth stations have large, sophisticated and highly reliable receiving dishes, even though the satellites transmitting such broadcasts are, in the main, of the low-power variety. But what about the viewer who is not on a cable network and may not be for some time to come and yet who still wishes to avail themself of such a wealth of entertainment? For such a person the only answer, at present, is to buy a Television Receiver Only (TVRO) system.

TVRO

There are a number of drawbacks to TVRO systems. The first is the cost; TVRO systems cost anywhere between £800-£1,500. The second is that the dish is large and you will require planning permission for it as it will probably be over 0.9 metres in diameter. Third, and perhaps more importantly, the dish has to be aligned extremely accurately. It must be located in a direct line with the horizon, more difficult the further north you go. There must not be anything obliterating its line of sight. Fine if you live in the country with few trees around but another matter altogether for the urban dweller. Fourth, the dish must also be fixed very securely; a slight gust of wind can blow it a fraction of a degree out of line and reception will be lost. This may not be so much of a problem for a dish fixed into the ground but on the roof it can be another story altogether! For more money, you can get a motorised dish which allows you to realign it in such circumstances and, really for ease of use, such a dish should be considered a necessity, particularly if you want to pick up transmissions from more than one satellite. Even then, the quality of the received transmission can leave a lot to be desired and the golden rule would seem to be that if the picture is not as good as, or better than, pictures received by conventional broadcasting means, then don't bother with a TVRO system! Understandably, TVRO systems have not really 'taken off' in a big way although some educational institutions have acquired what many regard to be the latest in 'yuppie' status symbols.

What does a TVRO system offer education and training? It is, after all, television by another route and only one-way communication at that. Although kits are readily available for a price, and the price is steadily falling, the educational enthusiast would claim that, for such things as foreign language study, media studies and current affairs, the advantages outweigh the disadvantages. Certainly, the functions of satellites in these respects cannot be easily achieved by conventional broadcasting. The potential also exists for using low-powered satellites and TVRO systems to deliver educational and training programmes to those engaged in open learning. But who will provide the kits, install them and maintain them? How many open learners, because of geographical location, would be able to receive such transmissions? Is the provision of an educational channel on one of the present low-powered satellites an economic reality? Would it not make more sense to use existing and conventional broadcasting or videotapes to achieve the same, more easily and cheaply?

In the next few years, we will be seeing, all being well, the launch of several medium to high-powered satellites for broadcasting purposes. It is these satellites which are generating much of the current excitement amongst the educational and training fraternity. Indeed, if it was not for this latest breed of satellites, many a prospective educational satellite user would have packed their bags a long time ago. The age of direct broadcasting by satellite is now dawning.

Direct
TVRO is direct broadcasting in the strict sense but the word has started to take on a new meaning because, with direct broadcasting by satellite (DBS), most people, should they want to, will be able to receive directly from the satellite high quality transmissions with greater ease and for relatively little cost. It is this prospect, along with other possibilities, that has got the tongues of some educational providers wagging.

Because the new breed of satellites will be transmitting at much greater power, not only will the footprint of the satellite be larger, ie transmissions will be over a larger geographical area, but also the size of dish required will be smaller. Estimates of dish size vary; figures quoted are in the range of 0.4 to 0.85 metres but under the 0.9 metres size for which planning permission is required. Due to the greater power of the transmission, the margin for dish misalignment is slightly wider than that of a TVRO dish but dishes must still be sighted with an accuracy of one degree or better, which means that they will also need to be motorised. Improvements and developments in transmission standards will lead to better quality pictures being received, with possibilities for stereo sound and data transmission being available at the same time; however, the former will largely depend on the transmission standard chosen.

A major consideration at the present time lies in the lack of agreement on transmission standards. The transmission standard MAC (multiplexed analogue components) is not the problem but the type of MAC to be used is. The type of MAC standard chosen is important because it will govern the type of microchips required in DBS receiving equipment. Get a receiving system with the wrong microchips in it and you may not be able to receive all satellite transmissions. The use of a MAC standard offers satellite users not only clear pictures but also several channels of digital sound which quality-wise are comparable to a compact disc.

Currently two MAC standards, D-MAC and D2-MAC, are front runners with different odds in different countries. C-MAC seems to have dropped out of favour, with 70% of the European market putting their support behind D2-MAC, mainly because there are more microchips available which are compatible with this standard. C-MAC carries eight channels of hi-fi sound (four stereo pairs) in conjunction with pictures. In this way, the same programme could be broadcast in several different languages, radio stations could piggy-back their broadcast programmes on the TV channels, and a sound channel could be shared between, say, industry and education in order to broadcast data and text. What more could anyone want? Unfortunately, some European countries objected to C-MAC because of its wide bandwidth which would not travel down their existing cable networks and, so, D-MAC was born.

D-MAC has the same number of hi-fi channels but, due to some clever digital coding tricks, operates in a narrower bandwidth. D2-MAC, on the other hand, only has four sound channels, so if you want to transmit eight channels with D2-MAC, then you will lose audio quality and end up with something which sounds little better than a medium or long wave radio broadcast!

In practice, all this means that, if you buy a receiving system with D2-MAC microchips in it, you won't be able to receive D-MAC signals. This will be important if British satellite broadcasters decide to use D-MAC, as looks likely at the present time. Although some firms are planning to sell microchips which can cope with both systems, these are not ready yet. So, if you feel compelled to rush out and buy the first DBS receiving system on the market, then caveat emptor!

However, the problem does not end with a system which contains the 'universal MAC microchip' because additional, specialised, microchips will also be required in order to unscramble encrypted transmissions, as most DBS programmes will have to be scrambled if the operators are to make any money out of the venture, as well as, in some cases, for reasons of confidentiality. The need for these additional microchips to de-encrypt satellite transmissions could add up to quite an increase on the retail price of a receiving system. The final decision, yet to be made by the satellite broadcasters on both counts, will not only have a profound effect on the availability of microchips but also on the different types of receiving equipment on sale in the shops. One thing is for sure, and that is until someone makes a decision then manufacturers cannot start to make DBS receivers and tuners with any degree of certainty. What interesting times we live in!

It has been estimated that in a couple of years you will be able to walk into your local hi-fi/electrical store and buy, off the shelf, a DBS system for around £300-£400. Whether this will pick up all satellite broadcasts remains to be seen! If, for the price, one equates what computers have done for open learners, then might one say the same about DBS systems? As with computers, the potential will be there but what will it take to realise that potential?

If DBS has the power to open up the reception of a vast number of broadcast channels, then educational providers may decide that an educational channel would make sound, economic sense, particularly if the reception of that channel was pan-European and other EEC countries were to use its facilities. Without a pan-European usage, it is difficult to see why the UK would want a DBS educational channel when it already under-utilises its more conventional means of broadcasting! However, such a channel would allow for the transmission of a large number of high quality learning materials right across Europe.

One of the high-powered satellites due for launch in 1989 is the European Space Agency's OLYMPUS-1. The ESA have agreed to allow free use of one of the two DBS transponders (transmitters) for nine hours a day to bona fide educational users over two years. In addition to the DBS payload, OLYMPUS-1 also carries a 'Specialised Services Payload' for communications between small earth terminals, and a 'Communications Payload' for point-to-point and multipoint teleconferencing and other experimental applications. Potential users can also bid to use one of these services as well which means that companies will be able to try new data services without paying for them but, after two years, commercial rates will apply. To many of those involved in education and training, such an offer was too good to miss but it soon became apparent as people started doing their sums that around 85% of the total costs of using DBS lay in the production of materials and associated services. Although 'air-time' is not cheap, it does not consume a lot of the cake; the problem really lies in getting enough funding for materials production, etc.

The following organisations in the UK have been given video transmission time on the DBS payload:

Acton High School
Aston University
Birkbeck College
Brighton Polytechnic
British Universities File and Video Council
Centre for International Studies
Clwyd TVEI Centre
Coventry Lanchester Polytechnic
Educational TV Association
Gwynnedd County Council
Heriot-Watt University
Manpower Services Commission
Oxford University Language Teaching Centre
Postgraduate Medical School (University of Exeter)
Royal College of Psychiatrists
Scottish Council for Educational Technology
The Open University
University of East Anglia
University of Edinburgh
University of Glasgow
University of London

The proposals from the above organisations cover a wide range of subjects and materials, from material for teaching languages based on European television programmes, postgraduate training in medicine, training in electronic engineering, to sending training videos to centres in the UK (cheaper than sending a vast number of tapes through the post) and for continuing education covering programmes on managing coastal zones and religious ideas.

All, of course, depends upon the successful launch and deployment of OLYMPUS-1 as there is no back-up satellite. But, if all goes according to plan and assuming that all the UK initiatives are evaluated in an objective and independent manner, in three years' time the educational and training world should have some very valuable information available upon which to base future decisions concerning the use of satellites in open learning.

One of the more exciting aspects included in several of the above projects is the use of 'two-way' communication. By using a two-way audio connection, either by terrestrial land lines or through the specialised services payload on OLYMPUS, along with one-way visual, a quasi form of two-way communication can be introduced. However, in our view, true, full two-way communication can only be obtained through video conferencing.

Video conferencing
Video conferencing can be viewed as an extension of DBS-type facilities with additional features. If money were no problem, you could arrange with British Telecom or Mercury for a video conference at the present time, using existing low-powered satellites. This form of communicating is used by large businesses and companies who argue that it is cost-effective, but they are starting from a higher cost threshold in the first place.

The question open learning has to address is whether video conferencing via high-powered satellites will be a viable option. The answer is not very promising. In the foreseeable future, it is likely that video conferencing will still be out of the range of most education and training institutions' budgets, as both production and transmission will remain costly. The situation is compounded by the need for very powerful, and at the moment expensive, uplinks in addition to DBS receiving equipment. It may be a different picture when the UK has a full Integrated Services Digital Network (ISDN), along which can be carried both sound and pictures to one uplink site, but that day is still some way off. ISDN, in the first instance, is designed for the business community and it is fair to estimate that it will not be until well into the 21st century that education can afford such facilities.

There are also additional problems with video conferencing, many of which are likely to be encountered by the use of direct broadcasting as well as one-way visual and two-way audio conferences. For example, the controls imposed in relation to privately owned Post Telephone and Tele-communications companies mean that monopolies and tariff structures govern European communications. In the UK, British Telecom and Mercury hold the monopoly over uplinks, so that anyone else who wishes to uplink to a satellite will have to go through either one or other of the companies first. The copyright laws in Europe do not make it clear about what may, or may not, be legally transmitted. In the UK, time zones are not a problem but, if you wish to have a video conference with a broad European market or for multipoint global transmissions, then consideration must be given to these. Other problematic aspects which cannot be overlooked are: the present lack of encryption and technical standards; language, cultural and political issues for pan-European links; and the flexibility that 'own time' delivery has for the open learner compared with the greater interactivity possible with 'real time' delivery.

Considerations for the future
Clearly, education and training is only at the shallow end of the satellite pool and indeed may not get any further! If open learning is to be in a position to assess and exploit this technology, then it will require some firm evidence upon which to base decisions. Case studies of educational use are required over the next few years to provide us with the answers to the following questions:

What are the costs involved?

What benefits are there for the learner?

What kind of 'telepresence' is needed to teach via satellite?

What types of interaction, reinforcement and support materials are needed to maximise learning in distance learning of this kind?

How are students motivated in this type of learning environment?

How easy is it to use; what range of equipment is required, how much technical support is needed?

Is it more beneficial and efficient than other methods of delivering open learning?

Only when we have answers to all these questions will we be able to put an end to all the hype and to say whether or not we have found a life-line for open learning.

11. Open learning, Information Technology and further education

Peter Trethewey

Further Education Unit (FEU)

Peter Trethewey is the director of the FEU Courseware Unit. The views expressed in this article do not necessarily represent the views of FEU.

Throughout this paper, it is assumed that open learning is valuable per se, since it increases student autonomy and offers increased access to learning.

The paper seeks to clarify the meaning of the term open learning and, in particular, its relationship to Information Technology. This is to be achieved by exploring the concepts involved on two main dimensions:

(i) The continuum from *informal* to *formal* education/training

(ii) The continuum from *no support* to *full support*.

In conducting this analysis, various definitions of open learning will be explored and other dimensions, such as institutional flexibility and cost, will emerge.

The formal/informal continuum

I am defining *formal* education/training (Fig 11.1) as a learning process designed by teachers, institutions and examination bodies to be delivered to students. Learning is then seen as a controlled process leading to validated standards of achievement. This is naturally the business of examining bodies and other national organisations concerned with education and training.

Informal to formal education/training

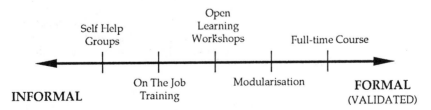

Fig 11.1 — The formal/informal continuum

81

Traditionally, this has been interpreted as the delivery of courses to full-time or part-time students at the college. Any flexibility in such a system depends to a large extent on successful precourse counselling, enabling appropriate course choices. Latterly, more flexibility has been implemented in such courses by allowing students increased access to such delivered courses through open learning workshops. Thus, the autonomy of the student has been increased by giving him/her more freedom concerning times of attendance and pace of learning. Another added benefit of open learning workshops is that the student is often more actively engaged in his/her own learning than would be the case in a traditional classroom.

However, the flexibility offered to students in the context of such delivered courses is often minimal. In essence, courses are offered on a 'take it or leave it' basis. With the growing popularity of modularisation, students may well have more flexibility concerning course content through processes of counselling and negotiation leading to choice of appropriate course modules. Such a situation provides a constructive compromise between the needs of students and the need for nationally recognised qualifications.

Although it is assumed that such delivered courses are often designed at colleges of FHE, there is of course no necessary commitment to deliver them through the authoring institution. A student can receive delivery of such a course through the postal service and this, of course, increases access to qualification. Any necessary tutorial support can then be provided by the most cost effective and convenient path for the student. This is one definition of open learning as popularly portrayed by the MSC through such initiatives as the Open Tech programme and The Open College.

At the other end of the continuum, I have placed *informal* education/ training. Here the individual may be firmly in control of his or her own learning and possess a very high degree of autonomy. Such a student need not necessarily be interested in qualifications but simply in, for example, how to wire his/her house. This need may be satisfied by borrowing a library book or watching a television programme. It also embraces what could loosely be termed the self-help group which comes together for some common aim/purpose. Such an example could be a group that decide to produce a community newspaper. I am implying that such a group or individual may or may not choose to be helped by nationally validated courses. The choice is entirely theirs.

We can also include much of what constitutes 'on the job' training under this heading. Validation of such learning experiences might well be possible but would almost certainly bring more formality to what, at present, may be perceived as a fairly haphazard process of learning. Such a development can be seen as more flexibility or openness on the part of examining bodies.

Those adults who wish to develop their own autonomy and for a variety of reasons do not wish to partake in the formal education process can be helped much earlier in their lives by ensuring that they have the necessary study skills that they may need in following up their own learning and interests.

However, if the problem is one of gaining easier access to education/training and the necessary support, there are many ways that information technology can help and these are briefly explored in the next section.

The no support/full support continuum
At one extreme, we can envisage the student/learner working alone with a textbook or television series. Often, incidentally, the situation that a teacher finds himself in when preparing a taught course. In this situation, peer group support might be very important, particularly if we are thinking of a self-help group.

A lone student may be considerably helped by studying prepared distance learning material. This usually consists of text based material, structured in such a way as to assist the student in the assessment of his own progress. Such text based open learning material usually has embedded in it a didactic linear teaching style of the teachers/authors. It may also have built into it varying degrees of tutorial support.

To increase motivation, learning effectiveness and efficiency, there has been development of multi-media distance learning material integrating, for example, text and video, typical of the Open University approach. To further advance motivation and student interactivity with the material and to help manage the learning process, there has been increasing interest in the use of computer based learning and, in particular, the use of interactive video with or without text based components.

There has often been a basic assumption in the production of the type of resource outlined above that, despite the large cost of producing this courseware, ultimately cost savings will be made by reducing the need for tutorial support to a minimum or even nil and similarly improving the efficiency of the learning, thus reducing length of study time.

As such resources become more sophisticated, there is no doubt that the richness of the learning experiences they offer will improve and less didactic

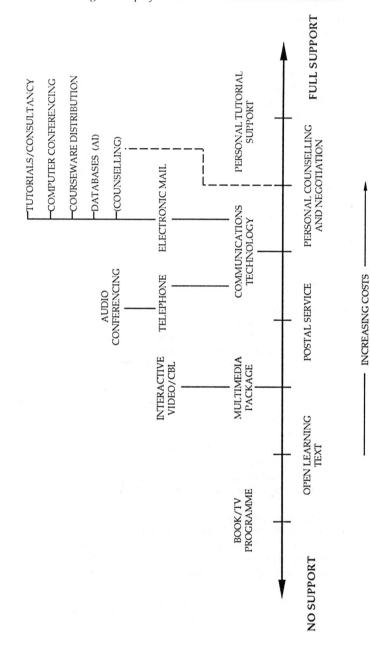

Fig 11.2 — No support to full support

teaching strategies will be used if appropriate. The development of Artificial Intelligence has, as one of its goals, the 'intelligent' work station able to model student performance and guide his or her learning processes. The beginning of such a system is already promised within the MSC's TAP (Training Access Points) initiative.

Sophisticated simulations and other types of computer based learning might well permit groups of learners or individuals to learn complex tasks without the necessary presence of a tutor. It can be argued that systems that seek to write out the need for tutorial support are naïve and doomed to fail. However, such support need not involve travelling and can be delivered wherever is most convenient to the student — at home, at the workplace or in a learning institution.

The postal service and the telephone are obvious and relatively cheap vehicles for tutorial support. The telephone in particular offers much potential for remote tutorial support. Audio conferencing has already been used to bring together widely dispersed students, either to deliver courses or aid the formation of self-help groups of professionals.

Electronic mail offers the big bonus of being time independent, so that messages can be left for electronic tutorials or consultancy. Groups of students can be electronically brought together via a computer conference for course delivery and/or mutual self-support. Such systems, because of their nature, do not distinguish between the institutions supplying help/ advice. Electronic tutors might reside within colleges, industry or be home based and the same, of course, is true for students.

Some developments promise the remote delivery of course material, be it text or courseware, over the telephone line or remote interactive video over fibre optic cable. One can envisage a national library of resources for training/education that could be available on demand. Remote electronic access to powerful databases might also provide support for electronic counselling. TAP has already been mentioned but MARIS, ECCTIS and POLYTEL have similar roles to fill.

It is worth remembering that any support with a live person at the other end, be it via post or telephone line, is going to produce a sudden increase in cost. The systems outlined, however, do offer some cost saving, due to reduction in travel costs, in increasing student access to tuition and support and in possibly reducing the need for large maintained buildings to house tutorial staff and students.

It is often argued that the use of communications technology, as outlined above, will not make a major impact on educational institutions. The reasons for this usually include the costs involved in giving staff increased access to telephone lines, the necessary hardware and the requirement for basic staff development in the use of such systems. However, such basic computing skills are often taken for granted in the larger companies and new staff will automatically receive basic training when joining the organisation.

It is tempting to suggest that there is a fundamental institutional block to such developments, since they can be perceived as threatening the vertical hierarchical communication structure firmly established within the institution. Conversely, those in society who might wish to change educational institutions might encourage horizontal electronic communication and, in so doing, disenfranchise such institutions from their student population in the subsequent deinstitutionalisation.

There is no doubt that open learning is most successful if supported by personal counselling and tutoring. It is, however, undoubtedly the most expensive option, since it involves the maintenance of buildings and the travel of students. There are, however, many learning experiences that can only be successful by bringing groups of students together under the guidance of a skilled tutor. Those relating to interpersonal skills, or the use of expensive equipment/facilities, are perhaps the most obvious.

I have brought together the two dimensions referred to in this paper in Figure 11.3 and attempted to place the various types of open learning on this matrix. In conclusion, I have tried to indicate the various ways open learning can be defined by different groups in society and the necessary conclusions on likely future developments that these different perspectives represent. Those seeking national validation for a wide population at minimal cost will explore all the potential that IT has for remote support and delivery, and such developments, if successful, are likely to deinstitution-alise or disperse education/training establishments. Those seeking to maintain the quality of the education/training are likely to insist on the obvious benefits of face-to-face tutorial support.

Colleges may wish to consider how they can open their resources and expertise to the wider clientele represented by those involved in informal education/training. The FHE system will come under increasing pressure to open its remit and to negotiate curricula based on the needs of local institutions/employers and, at the same time, may need to further widen this negotiation to include local community groups and individuals in need of support. Failure to change to this more open remit may mean the gradual erosion of institutions of further education by a subtle process of deinstitutionalisation.

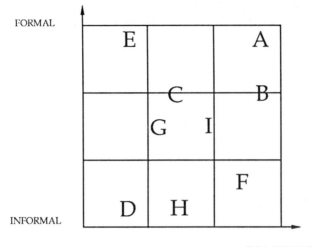

Fig 11.3 — The open learning environment

Student A — attends a full-time formal BTEC course.

Student B — attends an open learning workshop and is studying O-level maths with full tutorial support.

Student C — is studying for a vocational qualification at the workplace, with the aid of multimedia packages, including some computer based training and has access to electronic tutorial support.

Student D — has built up a lot of practical expertise in the repair of motor cycles from books, magazines and the circle of motor cycle enthusiasts to which he belongs. He is not interested in studying for exams.

Student E — is studying a correspondence course in O-level French with minimal tutorial help, *or* is a teacher preparing a traditional taught course which is new to him/her, through the preparation of notes from text books.

Student F — is undertaking research in an area of great interest to him for his PhD under the guidance of a supervisor who is also seen as a close personal friend.

Student G — is following an OU course in child care that uses a multimedia pack, no tutorial back-up and does not lead to qualification.

Student H — is learning a lot of new skills from his work supervisor but is not studying for any qualification.

Student I — is a teacher, one of a geographically dispersed group of teachers and trainers undertaking a course of staff development in the use of communications technology, through the use of computer and audio conferencing and occasional face-to-face meetings with the rest of the group.

12. Continuing education, computer mediated communications systems and open learning

Celia Graebner
Sussex University

1. Introduction

The preceding paper by Peter Trethewey has presented open learning as process — student-centred, autonomous but not necessarily unsupported — rather than the practice of providing off-the-shelf training. Accepting that interpretation, the present paper sets out to develop, from the particular perspective of community-based continuing education, some general guidelines and one possible model for exploiting the potential of computer mediated communications systems (CMCS) to extend access and opportunities for active — and interactive — open learning. Specific technologies referred to are all currently available.

2. Support needs for open learning

The problem of establishing effective support for open learning is complicated when Trethewey's formal/informal continuum of learning modes is taken into consideration. In practice, the two modes frequently intersect: the range of learning experiences taking place in and around a traditional face-to-face course may include significant informal components, for example when a tutor or student discusses the last course meeting with a peer. Equally, the priorities of an individual learner may move between the formal and the informal over time; the graduate of a formal course may subsequently need to consolidate his learning through informal discussion and evaluate his position with the help of an educational advice service, before settling on a new direction which requires further formal training. Perhaps the major challenge to the organisation of open learning in post-compulsory education is that of accommodating a plurality of modes of learning and of learning support and allowing for easy transition between them. If the new information technologies are to be effectively deployed to meet this challenge, the area of research into teaching and learning interactions with CMCS identified in Dick Davies' paper (page 67) is of crucial importance.

3. The problem of models for IT-based learning schemes

Clearly, though, the elements of the IT repertoire show great variation in their capacity to support a given kind of learning experience. By way of illustration, the established core elements of electronic communications systems are mapped in Figure 12.1 from the point of view of their potential for interactive learning.

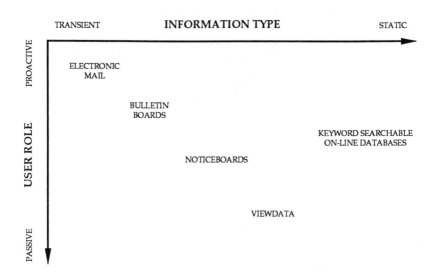

Fig 12.1 — Electronic communications systems and interactive learning

An appropriate choice of IT elements to support a particular open learning scheme will depend on prior targetting of its requirements in terms of learning interactions and styles.

Although it is sometimes claimed that the qualitative differences between information exchanges in CMCS and traditional communication systems make design inferences from existing structures irrelevant or misleading (1), as far as providers and researchers of new IT-based learning opportunities are concerned, there would seem to be strong practical arguments for starting from models of existing educational information exchanges:

> 'Without knowing the prior information flows and communication relations, one has no base case against which to compare the new, changed relations resulting from the implementation of the new technologies. This (lack of background) . . . also tends to draw the researcher into the role of myopic promoter of the new technologies.'

The following section will be concerned with delineating patterns of information exchange specific to open access community courses, which could provide a template for developing an appropriate CMCS system for small or isolated student groups. In the meantime, two criteria derived from traditional face-to-face learning might be posited as having general relevance for computer mediated open learning systems — a criterion of convivial scale:

'One of the basic principles of CMCS design should be to encourage relatively small task-oriented groups and communities of interest';

and a criterion of flexibility: if the system is to accommodate the varying needs of autonomous users over a period of time, it needs to be adaptable to a variety of types and levels of interaction.

4. Communication patterns in a student-centred course

The type of course under discussion will be community based but administered by a local co-ordinating agency — community education centre, FE college or university extramural department; its existence will be dependent on a minimum group size, usually in the region of thirteen to fifteen, which guarantees an acceptable level of fee income, and on the availability of a suitable (often freelance and peripatetic) tutor.

The distinctive patterns of these open access courses can be illuminated by setting them against those of formal continuing education, as represented by the short professional updating courses provided by the same agencies.

COMMUNITY COURSE	SHORT COURSE
Open access	Group specific
Student centred	Skill centred
Negotiated course content	Topic specific
Face-to-face teaching; usually single tutor	Face-to-face; range of tutors
Intermittent but usually extensive	Intensive but possibly
(10, 20 or 30 weeks)	recurrent

If we envisage translating both courses into CMCS supported open learning versions, the appropriate support structures are likely to be quite divergent. For example, while the planning, delivery and follow-up phases in the short course may correlate well with different selections from the CMCS repertoire, the negotiated nature of the community course precludes such differentiation.

At the snapshot level of the single two-hour session, a community course is likely to include a number of areas of information exchange, with varying principal actors (Fig 12.2). Given this range of interactions to model, highly specific IT systems would seem to be less appropriate and cost-effective than an adaptable and locally-controlled general-purpose communications system, with the possibility of mediated access to larger information retrieval systems.

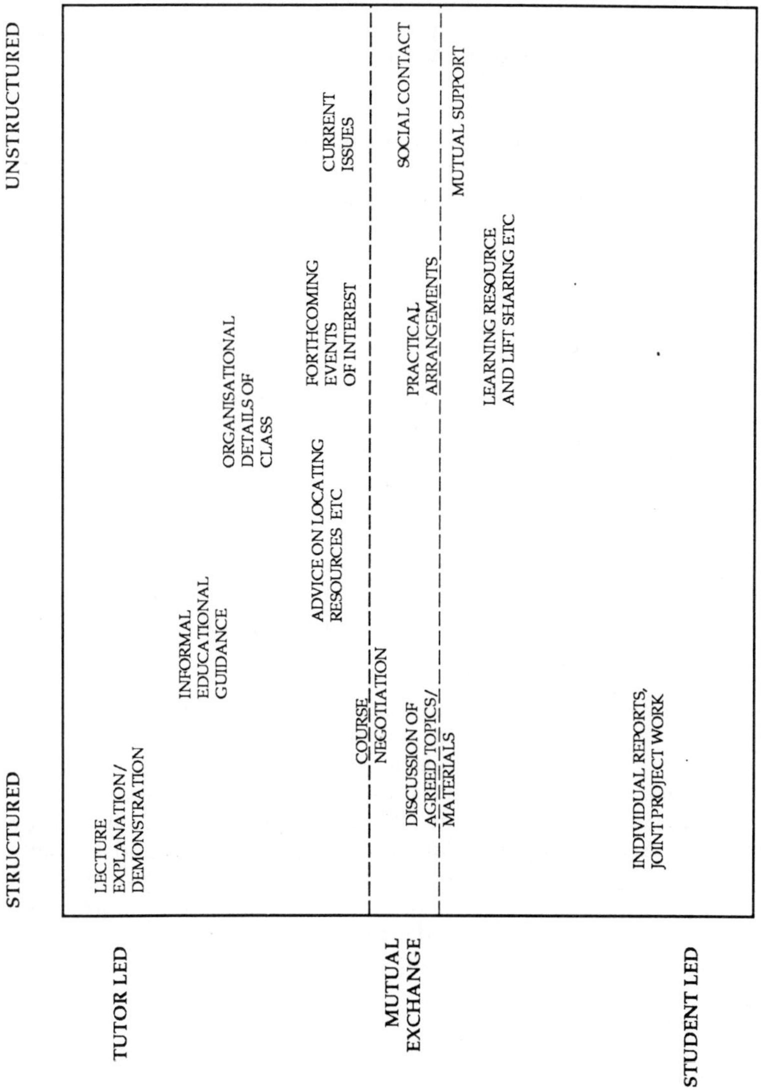

STRUCTURED   UNSTRUCTURED

TUTOR LED

LECTURE
EXPLANATION/
DEMONSTRATION

INFORMAL
EDUCATIONAL
GUIDANCE

ORGANISATIONAL
DETAILS OF
CLASS

FORTHCOMING
EVENTS
OF INTEREST

CURRENT
ISSUES

SOCIAL CONTACT

ADVICE ON LOCATING
RESOURCES ETC

COURSE
NEGOTIATION

MUTUAL
EXCHANGE

DISCUSSION OF
AGREED TOPICS/
MATERIALS

PRACTICAL
ARRANGEMENTS

MUTUAL SUPPORT

LEARNING RESOURCE
AND LIFT SHARING ETC

STUDENT LED

INDIVIDUAL REPORTS,
JOINT PROJECT WORK

Fig 12.2 — Interactions within a single session of a community course

5. Modelling student-centred learning — the potential of computer conferencing for continuing education

A unified CMCS environment of sufficient sophistication to support a range of learning needs is the computer-mediated conferencing system, already established on the North American continent as a delivery vehicle for distance learning.

In the UK, the lead in developing conferencing as an adjunct to distance learning has been taken by the Open University. An adaption of the CoSy system developed at the University of Guelph in Ontario is accommodated on the University's VAX system. Currently still at the experimental stage, it is scheduled to form an integral element of the new D220 Introduction Technology course in 1988, though not all the estimated 2,000 students taking the course will be included.

A few courses using conferencing are already under way: a postgraduate course in Educational Technology at the University of Bath and Hampshire's BTEC Business Studies course; both using the Open University's CoSy conferencing system, while the PART1 system has been used for an innovative communications course for FE tutors in the Hampshire Information Technology project.

The recent migration of well-developed conferencing software from mini-computer to microcomputer-based systems should make the establishment of independent 'in-house' conferencing a viable option for local colleges and centres (3).

Figure 12.3 plots the information needs laid out in section 2 of this paper against facilities provided by a typical conferencing system. Fully developed, with independent access to a microcomputer and modem for all participants, conferencing could provide a virtual learning centre, free of time and space constraints. The lateral communications facilitated by conferencing may open up new dimensions of independent and mutually supportive learning, providing opportunities for collaborative research and writing, and the formation of spontaneous self-help or information-sharing networks, and allowing disabled or housebound students to participate fully in a convivial learning group.

6. Some attainable goals

In the absence of the idealised fully-fledged open learning system sketched above, significant new learning opportunities can be derived from making conferencing available at regular intervals to tutors and groups of students through a local centre:

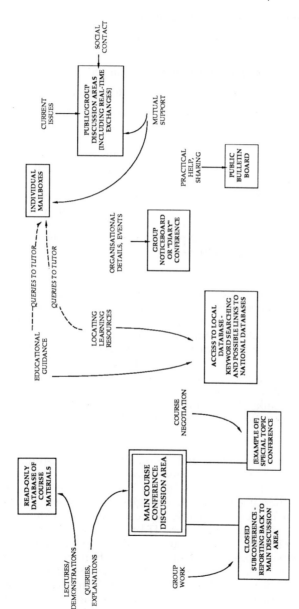

Fig 12.3 — Computer conferencing facilities in relation to structured/unstructured information exchange

- combining 2 or 3 small scattered groups into a viable class
- meeting separately with on-line tutor support and occasional face-to-face contact
- exchanging information with other similar groups
- electronic publishing (perhaps as a result of inter-group collaboration)
- formation of tutor contact groups, and improved tutor/host institution communication.

Even this level of provision still seems a long way off. It is not that the technical requirements are particularly exacting: for an outlying centre all that is needed is access to one of the many modems already provided to schools and colleges, and an agreement on covering the telephone charges incurred by student groups. The commitment required from a host institution would be at least part-time use of a personal computer with hard disk and modem, initial expenditure on software and some help with any necessary adaptations thereafter.

But, as with other new information technologies in education, a major barrier to diffusion is lack of direct experience among potential users — trainers and organisers as well as students. The first courses in the UK to adopt CMCS as an integral element have been in IT-based areas — Educational Technology, Computer-Aided Design, Business Studies — and almost all have been at graduate or undergraduate level. A fresh impetus towards the implementation of conferencing systems at local level may result from the current growth of CMCS in educational administration; once course providers accept conferencing as a means of building organisational links, its recognition as a teaching and learning resource for community education cannot be far behind.

Notes
1. See, for example, Hiltz and Turoff (1985), Structuring, Computer-Mediated Communication Systems to Avoid Information Overload, *Communications of the ACM*, Vol 28, No 7. On the other hand, where the learning medium itself is novel, analogies with familiar structures offer valuable initial reference points for users and providers. Successful innovative schemes for introducing IT-based learning and information to new users in Europe — such as the Scandinavian 'electronic village hall' initiatives, have exploited the advantages of building from the familiar. (*Social Experiments with Information Technology: Proceedings of the Odense Conference*, January 13-15, 1986, FAST Occasional Paper No 83, Commission of the European Communities.) In the educational world, the Times Network's very successful 'Newspaper Days' have drawn on a familiar

model to introduce the potential of electronic communications and publishing methods to teachers and pupils.

2. Melody, William H (1986), Learning from the Experience of Others: Lessons from Social Experiments in Information Technology in North America, *Social Experiments with Information Technology: Proceedings of the Odense Conference (ibid).*

3. A micro-based demonstration conferencing system has been running since late 1986 from the South Bank Technopark in London. The Mist+ software used on the Conexus system offers a full range of conferencing facilities: public and private conferences, an electronic mail system with on-line editing facilities, keyword-searchable bulletin boards and transfer of messages between conferences and to and from the mailing system (allowing for the setting up of sub-conferences or work groups). Useful features of the software are a choice of levels of help, to suit new and experienced users, and a readily adaptable source code.

The basic hardware requirements of the system are a dedicated IBM PC, XT, AT or compatible, with hard disk storage and appropriate modem; additional hardware is required to support multiple access.

PART IV

Case Studies

The four contributions in this section each deal with a different application of computer based communications media. Jane Cox and Valerie Campbell describe an experiment with desk-top publishing (reminding us that print is still a powerful medium!) for special needs students in further education. By contrast, Charles Crook and David McConnell tell of their experiences with electronic communications in undergraduate and postgraduate teaching, whilst Bridget Somekh and Susan Groundwater-Smith add an international dimension through their descriptions of links between the UK and USA, and UK and Israel.

13. Making a newspaper using a computer

Jane Cox and Valerie Campbell
Trowbridge College

1. Skills matching

a) The curriculum

The Assessment and Work Preparation course at Trowbridge College is for students with learning difficulties who, upon reaching 16, would be unable to gain full employment. Most come from special schools or support departments in comprehensive schools and have moderate learning difficulty. The course is for two years with two groups of eight students in each year, making 32 in total. In addition to this full-time course, school link courses are run by the Basic Skills department so that some students have been assessed over a year before arrival.

The course is serviced by approximately 30 members of college staff, both full and part-time. The core curriculum is timetabled as Communications, Numeracy, Workshop, Computer Aided Learning, Catering, Home Management, Art & Craft, Office Skills, First Aid and Family Care, PE and Swimming, Local Studies, Painting and Decorating. Options are Motor Vehicle, Electrics, Dress-making, Hairdressing, Environmental Studies, Horse-riding and DIY. In addition, there is a number of extra-curricular activities, including outdoor pursuits, work experience and residential periods.

The curriculum is more integrated and project based than this subject list suggests. In Communications, most time is taken up with newspaper production. Articles for the newspaper reflect activities from all other curriculum areas. Word processing skills to aid writing for the newspaper are taught in Computer classes. Numeracy and the hidden curricular social and personal skills are practised as students shop and keep stock records for Catering requirements. An annual factory simulation and regular markets integrate Workshop, Numeracy, Art, Office Skills, Catering, Local Studies and Computer Learning.

b) Profiling

Students at Trowbridge work with staff to complete the City and Guilds 3791 Profile. This profile can be used to cover a whole course or just one part of it, eg Newspaper Skills (see Appendix 3). All the skills categories apply, although some, like Writing or Working in a Group, have greater emphasis than others. Numeracy skills, for example, are only practised by students selling the papers. Regular up-dating of the profile by students and staff gives an oversight of the curriculum as a whole and specific monitoring of progress in curriculum areas like Newspapers. A separate article is published on Profiling at Trowbridge (1).

c) IT
Trowbridge College is a National Centre of Expertise for IT and Special Needs in FE after involvement in this field for a number of years. Belief in the value of the computer to aid learning for these students started the work. From 1985-7, Trowbridge was one of ten FE colleges taking part in a CET project 'IT for FE Students with Moderate Learning Difficulty'. Building on experience, the work continues. The college is well equipped in hardware and software as a result and the use of the computer as a tool for newspaper production was a natural step.

d) Employers
In 'Skills for the Future' (2), a Sheffield University research team found that employers rated personal qualities well ahead of five other categories at YTS trainee level. These personal qualities included ability to communicate, to mix with others and to work in a team. Successful newspaper production relies on such personal qualities.

2. Design of a student newspaper
a) Staff planning
The course team decided to start a newspaper because all students could contribute and gain satisfaction from seeing their work in print. The motivating aspects of writing with a word processor had been noted. The computer would offer a standard of printing, lay-out and graphics in newspaper production which would not be otherwise possible.

Newspaper production would practise skills like working in a team, making decisions and communicating which would satisfy curricular and employers' requirements. Assessment would be negotiated and on-going, using the City and Guilds 3791 profiling software.

b) Staff and student decisions
i.   Look at different newspapers published daily, weekly and monthly. Use the language of newspapers, eg headlines, Editor. Discuss the good and bad points of newspapers. Begin to form an idea of what the students' own paper should be like.

ii.   Compare different front pages and headlines; decide title and lay-out of proposed student paper.

iii. Discuss contents which might include stories, articles, reports, advertisements, competitions and pictures.

iv. Appoint Editor and discuss editorial job. Note that the lecturer remains Editor-in-chief!

v. Agree sharing time on the computer.

vi. Decide frequency of publication.

vii. Decide price, print-run and publication date.

viii. Discuss the fact that material submitted to the paper has to be approved. Should approval be the job of the Editor alone or a group decision with final Editorial say? If everyone has access to a word processor, the printed results can be given in for consideration. Trowbridge is fortunate in having enough work stations for everyone. If access is limited, write the article first and, if accepted, use the word processor to write up.

ix. Marketing: who sells the paper and collects the money; where to sell and who will buy it.

Implementation

a) Hardware

Trowbridge has BBC B and B+ computers with eight work stations on a Level 3 Econet system and a number of stand-alone machines with disk drives. Some software is better used on stand-alone machines because of ROM clashes, eg AMX Pagemaker is not available on a network system at present. Trowbridge does not use BBC Masters but problems with running software on these machines are well known. The Master's ADFS changed to DFS according to the instruction manual will help. If a particular piece of software still does not run, advice should be sought from Advisers, SEMERCS or the publishers of the software.

A printer is essential for making each page of the newspaper. Although a few copies can be run off using a printer alone, this is time-consuming and printing is on one side of the page only. A photocopier allows printing on both sides of the page and quicker, easier production of a larger number of copies.

b) Writing and word processing

Use of a word processor allowed students to correct their work easily, to save it on a disk or network space rather than on a scrap of paper, to lay it out pleasingly and see it printed out neatly. Students used Wordwise Plus as their word processor for writing their newspaper articles. They had user-space on the network system so they first had to type in a code to make the program work and allow them to save their writing. Teaching of word processing was in timetabled Computer Learning classes. Students were given a simple guide to using the program and a series of assignments to complete. When they came into class, they were given their personal record and each stage was ticked off. A Wordwise Certificate was given at the end of a set of assignments. There were three certificates altogether. Students found this approach motivating and the lecturer was always clear about what each student was working at and trying to achieve. These assignments and certificates are available on request.

Students reinforced word processing skills in writing articles for the newspaper during Communications classes. The Wordwise guides mentioned above were used if needed. Staff used them too.

When making a newspaper was being considered, some students were using Prompt for learning a sight-vocabulary. It was assumed that Prompt would be used by some students because Wordwise Plus was more difficult. However, all students insisted on writing with Wordwise. Perhaps they saw it as a 'proper' sort of word processor, used by more able students and staff. Wordwise is difficult for many because it relies on the red function keys for laying out the work. Using a guide, students achieved different levels of competence after practice. The other difficulty with Wordwise is that what you see on the screen is not how the work prints out. Initially, students tended to press 'Return' at the end of each screen line which spoilt the printed result, especially when corrections were attempted.

Spelling was a problem for some students. They either asked the lecturer or another student for spellings as they wrote, or relied on editing after finishing a part of the article. Romspell was tried as a spell-checker but, as it could not recognise homophone mistakes or proper names not in its dictionary, staff and students found it too time-consuming to go on with. Wordwise Dictionary Plus was more successful. This program enables the user to type the first letter or two letters of a word and press 'Shift/f2' to bring up a dictionary. Typing the code beside the chosen word brings it into the text at the right place. This can only work if the user knows the correct initial letter or letters and can read the words in the dictionary. Since the dictionary can be made totally individual, some preparation makes this a useful program for independent spelling.

What about students who cannot write independently? To write an article, they told the lecturer what they wanted to record. This was written out for them and they copied it on to the word processor. It could be argued that Prompt would have helped here but the time needed to make overlays for every article, perhaps to be used only once, which the student could not read anyway ruled it out. All students wrote on the same word processor and contributed articles. In the end, the fact that an article was short or had been done by copying words and having a great deal of help did not matter. Everyone had contributed and was pleased with the final results.

Some students became proficient at writing with Wordwise and could rattle off long articles, using all the embedded commands with ease to set their work out. Word processing gave confidence to previously poor writers and their articles became longer and used a wider vocabulary. There was no record of hand-written work from one student for his two years at college as he had systematically destroyed it all but he had 64 word processed files saved on his computer disk. Colleagues noted a general increase in self-confidence in many students as they succeeded in their work and considered that word processing contributed to it.

All teachers are familiar with the problem of the student who cannot think of anything to write. 'What are you going to write for the newspaper?' did not always bring immediate inspiration. Another consideration was that a newspaper does not need ten articles on 'Our trip to London' — it needs one. Trowbridge students are fortunate in the number of trips, work placements and residential experiences being run during any year. If there was really nothing obvious, comments were encouraged on news from local or daily papers. The sports, pop or fashion pages were helpful. Copying of articles was not allowed but re-writing in short was accepted.

Some students enjoyed making up their own 'stars', wordsearches, jokes and puzzles. There were computer programs to help with these: 'Riddles' enabled students to make up and print their own riddles. Wordsearcher helped with a wordsearch framework and this could also be printed out. Prizes were offered for competitions.

My FIRST is in
Rat but not in
Mouse

My SECOND is in
Cat but not in
House.

My THIRD is in
Abbot but not in
Costello

My FOURTH is in
Robert but not in
Fellow.

My FIFTH is in
Finish but not in
Fears

My SIXTH is in
Plant but not in
Ears.

WHAT AM I?

'Riddles' example

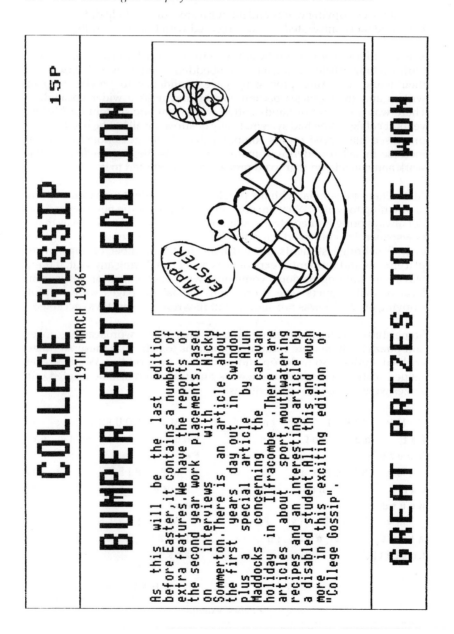

COLLEGE GOSSIP

15P

—19TH MARCH 1986

BUMPER EASTER EDITION

As this will be the last edition before Easter,it contains a number of extra features.We have the reports of the second year work placements,based on interviews with Nicky Sommerton.There is an article about the first years day out in Swindon plus a special article by Alun Maddocks concerning the caravan holiday in Ilfracombe .There are articles about sport,mouthwatering recipes and an interesting article by a disabled student.All this and much more in this exciting edition of "College Gossip".

HAPPY EASTER

GREAT PRIZES TO BE WON

c) Lay-out and desk-top publishing
The program Frontpage Extra was used for laying out the first front page of the students' newspaper. It was very easy to use and brought immediate and gratifying results. As well as making large headlines and sub-headings, boxes could be constructed for pictures. After persevering with the graphics in the program, they were abandoned in favour of sticking pictures into the box after the page was printed. The disadvantage of Frontpage Extra is that layout is as the program sets it. Trowbridge staff and students went on to AMX Pagemaker because it was more versatile. Fleet Street Editor was also available but it was considered too difficult to use. This was a pity as its 'Stars' graphics were superb. Frontpage Extra is a good program to start on. It is cheap, quick to bring results and any student who can manage the ordinary keyboard can use it. It does not require the fine manual dexterity of mouse-driven programs and people with the use of only one hand can be successful.

Trowbridge invested in AMX Pagemaker. This is a more complicated program because more than one disk is used and it is mouse driven. The red function keys can be used instead of the mouse but this is a slow process. The user has to point the mouse to different icons or symbols on the screen to make the program work. Staff wondered how many of the students would cope with it as they themselves took some time to learn the basics and needed considerable practice before mastering some of the finer points. One student, not noted for any particular dexterity or skills in any other field, was immediately at home with AMX Pagemaker. Working with icons came naturally to him. He was elected Editor of one of the two student newspapers because everyone was so impressed with his skills. He became responsible for lay-out in his paper and was the person who had to call in certain types of articles to fit his design. This student helped other students to use the program and was also consulted by staff when they had forgotten aspects of procedure. Other students were taught to use the program and they managed with varying amounts of help. Regular practice was needed to be successful.

The different fonts of Pagemaker were immediately attractive. Some news-papers were printed using a variety of fonts.

As the Trowbridge production line became more experienced, it was agreed that 'ordinary print' was preferable to fancy fonts because its size and uniformity made it easier to read. Fonts were reserved for the headings. Wordwise texts can be brought into Pagemaker and printed out with whichever font is chosen. Disks containing new fonts, including smaller ones, are now available for Pagemaker but were not when Trowbridge started using it. This procedure of using Wordwise texts in Pagemaker

THE COLLEGE GOSSIP

WHITSUN EDITION

CONTENTS

A DAY OUT IN BRISTOL

WHATS ON IN ILFRACOMBE

PROBLEM PAGE

ALL ABOUT MANDY

STORY BY NICKY

EXAMS

caused staff and students the most problems. The text has to be 'spooled' before it can be used, ie the green writing embedded commands have to be removed. If the text was too long, it ran off the page and spoilt the headlines set up by Pagemaker. Texts saved on network had to be downloaded to disk for use on the stand-alone AMX work station. Sometimes students had used Wordwise on the network without typing in their code and, in trying to save their work, lost their writing. When deadlines were imminent, Trowbridge must have resembled more eminent press offices in the levels of anxiety raised! At times, the heading was written with Pagemaker, saved and then, keeping the paper poised in the printer, an ordinary print-out of Wordwise was added.

d) Graphics
Graphics have not been a strong point in newspaper production at Trowbridge. Derby, one of the ten CET Project colleges, has used Image with admirable results (see Appendix 1). Trowbridge first relied on sticking in pictures or students' own illustrations. When AMX brought out 'Extra Extra!' disks with illustrations to use with Pagemaker, these were a welcome addition to later newspaper versions.

The RH Video-digitiser was available at Trowbridge and digitised pictures of the authors accompanied their newspaper articles. To use a video-digitiser, a special modem is needed, plus a video recorder and camera. These are attached to the computer and the pictures taken are printed out by the computer. The pictures saved on disk feed into AMX Pagemaker like the Wordwise files and can be cut and pasted, stretched or squashed within the program. Students enjoyed using the video-digitiser and liked to see their 'photos' in print. Since many colleagues would have use of a video-recorder and camera in college, the main expense to be considered is the cost of the modem.

e) Decision-making and the Editorial role
The processes of negotiation over content, lay-out and policy over newspapers have been valuable learning experiences. Students sat round the table regularly to discuss articles. It was interesting to note how the students coped with being told their articles were unsuitable or yet another wordsearch was surplus to requirements. The language of tact was introduced and the lecturer taught the students how to express unpalatable truths. From 'rubbish', they learnt to criticise kindly but firmly. Strong characters tried to dominate proceedings. One student wrote a horror story which made the staff feel sick but the other students were afraid to offend him by expressing similar views held privately. Here, the lecturer had to take over the Editorial role and persude the group to ask for moderation.

Blackpool Here We Come

On July 6th we are going to Blackpool with Jill and Jean. There will be 8 going from the unit for the holiday.

We hope the weather will be fine with lots of sunshine.

When we go to Blackpool we are going to stay in a guest house which is a long walk from the beach .

by

GAIL

Life at Elizabeth Lodge

At Elizabeth Lodge there are 6 people,4 girls and 2 boys. In the bedrooms there are sinks, cupboards and drawers. I started going to Elizabeth Lodge on the 16th of July 1986 and now there are 5 girls. Last night all the Elizabeth Lodge went to St Johns Church to have a Harvest lunch and after we had our lunch we got a singing book each and sang some songs,then after we sang some songs we all gave three cheers to all the people who played their instruments at St Johns church.Also the man gave us a bunch of flowers to take home.When we got home we put the flowers into a jar then we watched the television and after I watched some television I when to my bedroom and I did some of my cross word and now we have another person at Elizabeth Lodge.He is a boy and his name is Adam. Last night I was listening to my tapes.

written by Tracey Oakey

Two newspapers were always in production, one for year one and one for year two. They were published half-termly and the print-run of each was about 30. In the second year, the Editor was a student respected for her ability to write well and express strong opinions. She influenced group decisions about content and asked students to work on the articles they had promised. When the deadline was in sight, this Editor was well-organised and knew what work had to be completed and by whom. She rallied up the stragglers and made them finish their work on time. Not being a Pagemaker user, she set tasks for the students doing headlines and lay-out. Her team worked well.

In year one, the Pagemaker expert acted as Editor as the other students respected his skills in using it. He did not have organisational ability to start with, being a rather pleasant, easy-going personality who had never bullied anyone in his life. He certainly grew daily in self-confidence and began to organise the articles he wanted for Pagemaker. He was also asked to train other students in using Pagemaker so some work could be delegated to the one other machine fitted with the program. At first his 'teaching' was working the program in all its complex detail and giving a running commentary to the bemused onlooker. With help, he learnt to explain each part, giving his trainee small amounts of information and hands-on experience. But it was his patience when the production room became fraught that was really impressive.

Newspaper production showed how the students worked in a team. It forced isolated students to communicate and taught everyone how to approach each other. Students were working for a purpose and the deadlines set for production, with the attendant pressure, simulated situations at work.

f) Final production and marketing
When the pages were ready, the students collated them according to a previously agreed lay-out. The first editions were photocopied, which brought two problems to light. First was the quality of the reproduced pages. The Trowbridge printers had considerable use and an elderly ribbon contributed to rather faint print. A double strike code was later adopted in Wordwise to ensure bold print. The second problem was the time needed on the overworked college photocopier. With a queue of staff waiting for their turn, it became obvious that it was not a job students could be sent to do independently or at busy times.

Growing more ambitious, Trowbridge wanted printing on both sides of the paper. Collation of A4 sheets into the final edition proved a puzzle for everyone! Next, Trowbridge wanted folded sheets like proper newspapers.

This meant sticking A4 sheets on to A3 sheets and copying on to A3 paper on the photocopier.

A student was put in charge of sales and marketing of the product. Each copy was 10p, 15p or 20p depending on its size and quality. One edition contained the only definitive list of clothing requirements for the annual residential holiday so all the students were keen to buy a copy. The competitions were popular with a group of students and items such as an Eastenders Quiz were done at home by students and their families.

g) Staff development
A period on Monday afternoons in the first year was set aside for staff development, unless pressing engagements took precedence. Wordwise was practised and the guides were made, the first being on basic requirements like centring a heading. The second guide introduced more complex commands like tabulation. The manuals 'Introduction to Wordwise' and 'Wordwise Plus Reference Manuals' are both excellent but were found more useful when a basic knowledge of the program was attained. It was much more difficult to produce a simple guide to Pagemaker because of the complexity of the program.

Trowbridge staff worked by the cascade method, starting with the Head of Section who was very experienced in the use of IT. Because one lecturer was seconded full-time to the CET project, there was opportunity for supporting classes and availability for quick reference which would not normally happen in colleges. But it was the lecturer dealing with newspaper production who decided which programs were most useful and what was needed. She did not want to use programs which only staff could work. Fleet Street Editor was abandoned for this reason. At first, staff and one or two students learnt Pagemaker together and progressed together. The staff's teaching experience, combined with the students' technical ability, formed a team to train others, both staff and students. Echoing the national scene, new desk-top publishing programs appeared and new approaches were suggested. A flexible attitude was needed by staff in deciding to try out unfamiliar software, to take it up or reject it. Experience at Trowbridge suggests that newspaper production using IT would be stressful for staff who want to be seen as a fount of all knowledge and technical ability or who are unwilling to move with new developments in both hardware and software.

h) Student progress
Few students came to the college with much IT experience. One or two had Sinclair Spectrums at home on which they played games. Several families had computers in the house and again, games were played. It was not

thought important to teach touch-typing as it would take up too much time and the manual dexterity required was too demanding for the majority. These students with moderate learning difficulty would not have had the command of English to type quickly anyway.

Student progress with Wordwise and Pagemaker has been described above. Familiarity with the keyboard was practised with the program 'Keyboard' from the Microspecial pack.

The most noticeable area of progress was in the personal and life-skills involved in working as a team to produce a newspaper. Students learnt to be more assertive, to approach people tactfully to get their own way, to work to a schedule and to accept responsibility.

i) Assessment and profiling
At the start, the full curricular implications of making newspapers were not realised. Baselines of attainment were easily established for the communications skills of reading, writing, speaking and listening. A general comment about the students' personalities was recorded rather than detailing specific aspects. The City and Guilds Profile 3791 provided a useful framework for assessment and could be used for newspapers as well as for a whole course profile (see Appendix 3).

4. Evaluation
a) Review of the Trowbridge newspaper project
The skills needed for newspaper production involved all the categories of the City and Guilds Profile, so fulfilling the curricular needs of Trowbridge students with moderate learning difficulty. Employers want employees with the ability to communicate, to mix with others and to work in a team. Newspaper production practised these personal qualities.

Good points about the work were:

i)   All the students contributed.

ii) Progress in IT skills improved students' self-confidence.

iii) Criticism, assessment and decision-making were natural and essential parts of the process rather than simulations.

iv) Students learnt to work in a team.

Drawbacks of the work were:

i)   The lecturer teaching Communications felt that newspapers took up too much of the time allocated so that parts of the course were not covered.

ii) Wordwise was too difficult for some students who needed a great deal of support. The problem of pressing 'Return' after a screen line end persisted.

iii) Bringing Wordwise files into Pagemaker was problematic.

b) Next steps at Trowbridge

i) Communications, including newspaper production will be given more time on the course.

ii) Wordwise will be replaced by two word processors: Interword and Pendown. Interword is WYSIWYG (What You See Is What You Get) and the problem of pressing 'Return' at the wrong time will disappear. Interword also has screen instructions rather than relying on embedded commands alone. Staff and students have found it easier to lay out a page with Interword than Wordwise, eg tabbing is much simpler to do. There are some drawbacks to Interword: only about two pages can be saved on a 32K computer although there is a multifile option; some users find the smaller print of Interword tiring on the eyes; Interword will not feed into AMX Pagemaker and is not yet fully compatible with the Econet system. Nevertheless, its ease of layout largely compensates for these drawbacks. Pendown with its own special fonts will allow students who cannot cope with Pagemaker to make attractive headings. The dictionary facility, allowing the user to put his own words into it, will help with spelling, enabling less able students to produce better work more easily. It looks more professional than Prompt and initial student reactions are favourable.

iii) Image will be investigated for newspaper graphics.

iv) Staff are investigating the programs Communitel and Rotaview which download teletext pages through Prestel. Trowbridge hopes to learn from Bournville College in Birmingham, one of the CET Project colleges which uses Communitel with students with moderate learning difficulty. Using the framework of a page, students have altered pages and printed them out.

v) Students are beginning to work on the desk-top publishing program on an Apple Mac computer.

References
1. *Profiling FE Special Needs Using a Computer*, available from Trowbridge College.
2. Donaldson, Michael et al, *Skills for the Future*, Education Division, Sheffield University, Arts Tower, Sheffield S10 2TN (£5.00).

Appendix 1 — Magazine production at Derby

Garnet Wood from Derby College of FE, one of the ten CET Project colleges, describes magazine production by students on a Multiskills course:

Fleet Street Editor

Two of the students were very able on the computer and I spent some time showing them how to use this program. It is quite complex to operate and demands a fair amount of expertise. Certainly, the majority of our students would be unable to handle the program. It took about six hours before the two were reasonably competent in its use. The Wordwise files produced by the group were then loaded into the program and graphics from the graphics library, including headline fonts, were added to produce a completed article. In this way, a magazine of the London trip was produced. The students were really pleased and enthusiastic about the results and wanted to add other articles. Other groups, on seeing the work, also wanted to become involved and so, very rapidly, the London magazine expanded into a group magazine. It proved a tremendous incentive to producing written work throughout the whole of the Multiskills course. Throughout the project, it has become apparent that the more polished and professional looking the final product, the more time and effort the students were prepared to put into the work. Fleet Street Editor produces very professional and sophisticated results and the students were prepared to edit and revise their work a number of times in order to produce the desired standards. Overall, the standard of work was excellent.

Since all the articles and graphics needed to produce one page of Fleet Street Editor have to be collected together on one disk, this involves a considerable amount of disk organisation. The two students involved were quite capable of copying programs from one disk to another but selecting and copying proved very time-consuming. In the end, I did about three-quarters of the copying myself.

The printing in Fleet Street Editor is very condensed and some students were disappointed when all their efforts produced only a small area of print. However, there is a facility to spread the text and this was used to overcome this problem. The resulting text proved very difficult to read but none of the students seemed to mind this! Perhaps it was the lesser of two evils.

Image

Image was first used to design a poster advertising the London trip. The students were able to handle the main features of the program very quickly and the timely arrival of a colour printer ensured that enthusiasm was maintained. A cover was designed for the magazine and two short sessions were spent with a video linked to the program via a digitiser. This produced some very interesting results and gave rise to other possible applications which we hope to use in the future. The sessions were valuable in developing confidence, co-operation and language developments and, by the end, those involved were able to connect up and operate the various necessary elements. A video picture was used for the frontpiece of the London section of the magazine.

Appendix 2 — AMX Pagemaker at Clwyd

Alan Nevitt at N E Wales Institute, Clwyd used AMX Pagemaker with students with moderate to severe learning difficulty. With support from Alan to set up Pagemaker, his students chose the fonts and illustrations to set their writing off to the best advantage. All the students contributed to a final production called 'Past, Present and Future at the Unit'.

Appendix 3 — City and Guilds 3791 profile of newspaper skills

Talking and listening
Can communicate effectively with various people in work situations, eg asked students to contribute various sorts of articles such as reports, stories, puzzles. Discussed these with staff.

Writing
Can write reports describing work done, eg wrote newspaper articles on becoming confirmed and about his holiday experiences in the USA.

Reading
Can read various forms of written materials, eg read articles from other students, directions of using AMX Pagemaker, word processing guides and CEEFAX news.

Using signs and diagrams
Can interpret diagrams containing numerical or technical information unaided, eg interpreted the screen icons on AMX Pagemaker with minimal initial help and explained these to other students and staff.

Computer appreciation
Can enter data or text into existing programs, eg brought in Wordwise files, different fonts, cut-outs, pages and screens to use in AMX Pagemaker.

Using equipment
Can set up and use equipment to produce work to standard, eg set up BBC computer, checking the AMX Rom was in it, attached mouse and checked printer controls to produce paper.

Numeracy
Can solve problems by adding/subtracting whole numbers, eg sold newspapers and took the money.

Creating
Can produce a number of related ideas without help, eg set headlines, choose suitable fonts and arranged pictures using the 'Cut and Paste' and 'Clear and Define' icons.

Classifying
Can use tree-like classifying systems, eg accessed his own and others' word-processing files by using passwords for the user-space on the Econet system.

Working in a group
Can be an active and decisive member of a group, eg acted as Editor for the first year students' newspaper, asking for contributions and leading discussions on inclusion.

Working with clients
Can carry out clients' requests without guidance, eg carried out newspaper group's plans for particular lay-out and presentation of different articles and illustrations.

Accepting responsibility
Can follow a series of instructions independently, eg worked on his own as Editor and main user of AMX Pagemaker to use all the complex functions to make pages.

Planning
Can modify/extend given plans/routines to meet changed circumstances, eg planned newspaper lay-out after discussion with staff and other students. Organised his time in class to meet deadlines.

Obtaining information
Can use standard sources of information without help, eg used CEEFAX, newspapers, London guides and reference books to produce articles and check facts in others' contributions.

Assessing own results
Can assess own results/work with guidance, eg accepted advice about how to teach Pagemaker and began to teach in smaller steps, explaining carefully in more detail.

Coping
Can cope with unexpected or unusual situations, eg maintained good humour and persevered through program bugs, lack of correct scrolling, video breakdown, losing files, etc.

Appendix 4 — Notes on resources

Frontpage Extra
Publishers: MAPE, 76 Sudbrooke Holme Drive, Sudbrooke, Lincs LN2 2SF: £75 licence to LEAs.

AMX Pagemaker
Publishers: AMX, 166-170 Wilderspool Causeway, Warrington WA4 6QA: £79.95 for AMX Mouse Package (16k ROM and disk), £49.95 for AMX Pagemaker, £24.95 for Extra, Extra! disk.

Wordwise Plus
Publishers: Computer Concepts, Gaddesdon Place, Hemel Hempstead, Herts HP2 6EX: £39.81 for ROM chip.

Interword
Publishers: as for Wordwise Plus: £49 for ROM chip, £39.20 if you already have Wordwise.

Pendown
Publishers: Logotron, Dales Brewery, Gwydir Street, Cambridge CB1 2SF: £34 for a disk. An additional disk called Toolkits provides another 12 fonts.

Wordwise Plus Dictionary
Publishers: Nottingham University: £12.50 for the disk.

Romspell
Publishers: Watford Electronics, Jessa House, 250 Lower Street, Watford, Herts: £34 for ROM chip and disk.

Video-digitiser
Makers: Watford Electronics — see above: £109 for digitiser unit, software and manual.

Riddles (part of Dragonworld)
Publishers: 4Mation, Linden Lea, Rock Park, Barnstaple, Devon EX32 9AQ: £18 for disk.

Wordsearcher
Publishers: BLUEFILE: free.

Ceefax, Prestel, Communitel
Ceefax: Teletext Adapter £95.
Prestel: Modem from £75 upwards from Watford Electronics and other firms. Prestel users register with British Telecom, paying an annual charge. There is also a user charge. Check if your college is a registered user.
Communitel: 189 Freston Road, London W10 6TH: £55 for Level 1. A Prestel modem is needed.

Fleet Street Editor
Publishers: Mirrorsoft, Maxwell House, 74 Worship Street, London EC2.

Image
Publishers: Cambridge Micro Software, Edinburgh Building, Shaftesbury Road, Cambridge CB2 2RU: £39.95.

City and Guilds 3791 profiling software
Apply to: City and Guilds, 76 Portland Place, London W1N 4AA (Tel: 01-580 3050). A registration fee is paid for each student. An FE special needs version is available from Jane Cox, Trowbridge College, College Road, Trowbridge, Wilts BA14 0ES (Tel: 022-14 66241, ext 56).

14. Electronic media for communications in an undergraduate teaching department

Charles Crook
Durham University

Background

In October 1985, the Board of Studies in Psychology at Durham University agreed to explore the possibility of establishing a computer network to enhance communications within the department. It was hoped that this resource would prove of special value to administrative and teaching activities. A further decision was made to evaluate the effectiveness of such a network, leading to the presentation of case study material that could assist the university in making longer term plans for distributed computing on its campus. Thus, during the academic year 1985-6, various aspects of communication within the department were monitored to provide some modest baseline material against which to compare the network intervention.

Opportunity for communication through this network began in the 1986-87 academic year. The present report is a brief account of progress towards the end of this first year. Although activity has been monitored in some detail (see below), for this report, it will be necessary to rely more on the summaries of a participant observer (the present writer), supported by occasional reference to quantified observations that have been partially analysed where possible.

I shall first describe the setting up of the network and the present level of access. I shall then describe initial experience in the use of these resources within the department. Finally, I shall offer some commentary derived from the experiences of one academic year's communication.

The nature of the network

The department mainly teaches three-year honours and joint honours degrees in Psychology. It was decided to aim for a network that would be available to all teaching, research and technical staff as well as postgraduates ($N=6$), second year undergraduates ($N=41$) and third year undergraduates ($N=35$). The department also service teaches on a variety of Combined and General degrees: these students were excluded from the network, partly because they did not take a compulsory second year course 'Introduction to Computing' (traditionally statistical package work). Various teaching situations in which these students are mixed with Honours students has proved a persistent difficulty.

119

The department had already made a heavy investment in BBC micros for practical teaching, word processing and laboratory work. Given that mailer facilities do exist for network BBCs, some consideration was given to building the network around an Acorn Econet. However, it was judged that a greater degree of computing power might be necessary to attract full participation in this activity. For the same reason, it would be important to ensure that students had reliable access to the network at locations other than the Psychology building itself. Thus, it was decided to work through the facilities of the principal university mainframe service (an Amdahl V8 running MTS). The computer centre agreed to extended access for the Psychology department (to 28 2400 baud lines) and an increase in the number of registered users. The department purchased a minicomputer to function as a NIM for this connection and invested in Amstrad 1512 PCs as word processors and terminals for staff and secretaries. Other members of the department gained access, mainly through Televideo terminals or microcomputers with terminal emulators.

Access to the mainframe facilities are also available in the Computer Centre of the University, in the University library, in many of the student residences and through telephone links. Academic staff made a commitment to log on at least once during each day that they were in the department. Students were encouraged to make full use of the facilities and not to suppose that there were any constraints on who may be communicated with over this medium. Second year students took a traditional computing course which focused on developing fluency with statistical packages but which also provided tuition in using the messaging system. Third year students would have done this course in the previous year, although they would not have had attention drawn to messaging: printed instructions were given to this class, along with the same degree of encouragement to take part.

The message system on MTS is fairly sophisticated. It is possible to define group names exclusive to defined cultures of users (such as ourselves); messages can be forwarded; held for release until a given date; destroyed after a given date; a notice can be defined that alerts an incipient sender that you are away; whether and when a message has been examined by a recipient can also be determined. It is possible to have 'conversations' on-line and a facility exists to determine who, from a defined user group, is logged on at any moment.

Reasons for development
There were two reasons for wishing to mobilise this facility for undergraduate teaching. The first was an apparent failure of our existing teaching to arouse a sympathetic response to Information Technology and its application. The

second was a belief that the network could serve to develop educational practice in ways that we thought appropriate.

We discovered a negative attitude to computer use through the administration of a questionnaire designed by Dr Rosemary Stevenson to scale attitudes to computers. Not only was there limited enthusiasm for using the technology but, after our own efforts to introduce a basic computer literacy, attitudes were found to have hardened in a more negative direction. It therefore seemed appropriate to try and work computer usage more into the mainstream of the curriculum — allowing it to serve purposes with strong face value. This suggested the development of communication potential.

Our second purpose was to enhance the extent of student-student collaborations and the extent of tutorial contact with staff. This we believed was possible through liberal use of conferencing and messaging facilities. We had collected data concerning student working practices on course assignments that suggested students failed to make use of their peers as learning resources and that tutorial contact outside of the official seminar periods was very scarce.

Evaluation: methods
Our strategy for evaluating the progress of this initiative can be divided into monitoring that occurs either on or off the computer itself. That is, diaries, questionnaires and informal reports have been gathered along with the computer's own logging of system use. There are important issues of privacy relating to the latter strategy. Our approach has been to be quite clear that monitoring the use of various local facilities is part of the price for using them. However, the file into which the information is placed is on the account of a user with no involvement in the department and that user recodes the user identity information so that the privacy of individuals may be respected at the time of data analysis.

Evaluation: some initial experience
The availability of the system has proved popular with both students and staff. That is, there is good evidence that it has been widely and regularly used. System logs reveal this and accounts elicited from users are generally positive. However, from the point of view of the various participants, it would seem that it has had limited impact on teaching activities.

For staff, it is most widely used for routine administrative matters — arranging meetings and gathering information necessary to discharge various duties. For students it has been largely used in a fairly playful spirit to reinforce social contacts within the class. These comments can be expanded with respect to the three main categories of computer resources: databases, conferencing and message facilities.

The main database facility has been a menu-driven package that supervises all the reading lists and lecture handouts associated with various courses. It has been the responsibility of staff to channel material in this direction and it must be said that there remain significant gaps in this database. The centralisation of teaching material in this way has not been universally perceived as a high priority. This incomplete character of the database is likely to detract from its appeal.

The conferencing system has been a singular failure. It must be stressed, however, that the user interface for this program is very poor and most users have given as their reason for disliking the system the problems they have experienced in getting started. However, the feedback of three student practical class groups who attempted to use it systematically suggested that it did not serve a useful purpose in supporting their work.

The use of messaging has in some ways been more successful. At least, the usage has been quite active. But, again, it is not clear that it has served a potent role in strengthening teaching and learning practices as they stand.

In respect of student-tutor contacts, it must be said that the flood of messages that some academics feared from this medium has not occurred. This does not reflect lack of use of the system. One measure of activity that I have devised might be termed the 'half life' of a message: the number of working days (9am-5pm) which pass before half the members of some mail group have read a message. For second year students, this is in the order of 1.5 days (for staff it is approximately 2 hours). Third year students have been far less active and this seems to reflect a lack of conviction that the resource would be worth their effort at mastering it in a situation where instruction is not part of any scheduled class. However, the level of take-up by second year students suggests that their modest use of electronic mail for student-staff contact means either (i) existing practices furnish adequate interpersonal contact, or (ii) existing relationships do not encourage the easy use of the medium. One hopes there is some truth in the first possibility but our baseline (diary) measures of the frequency of face-to-face contact suggest that this is unlikely to be an important factor. The second possibility identifies obstacles that arise from the character of student-staff relations as they currently exist: this may be more significant. Certainly, there is evidence that student-student mail has been fairly active, even in a situation where students see each other fairly regularly.

In respect of both seminar and practical work, a similar situation prevails. There is only a limited spontaneous use of electronic mail for discussion, inquiry or instruction. The system *has* proved valuable for more administrative purposes in these contexts (eg, timetable changes, supplementing references) but it has not played a significant part beyond this.

Commentary
Firstly, the lack of extensive use for student-staff contact must be judged against some understanding of the character of the student-staff relationship as it has traditionally been established. Cursory examination of some of the electronic student communications that did take place suggests that they were largely inquiries with clear face validity: say, requests for some unambiguously legitimate information. The circumstances for more casual, diffuse and spontaneous inquiries do not seem to be well established.

Secondly, the failure of the medium to be widely used in supporting seminar-type work must be judged in the context of our observations of how this work was managed on a typical occasion within the previous year. It was clear from these records that practices had not been established for consulting with tutors within the period that work was being prepared. Neither, incidentally, was there much evidence of peer collaboration over such work. The implication is that, for electronic communications to function in these contexts, the participants have to *plan* things: the presence of the medium is not, in itself, adequate to promote a new pattern of communications. So, for example, in the case of a seminar essay, a structure has to be negotiated that supports the management of such work: it might be suggested that students submit rough outlines of their intentions as electronic messages and the tutor and/or other students could comment on these. There is little doubt that this strategy would fill a gap. Again, from our observations, normal working practices for this kind of assignment lack this kind of structuring: students typically do the bulk of the work within a short period very close to the deadline. The point is that electronic mail may need to be cultivated with the support of new patterns for organising the instructional process. It is not adequate to provide the infrastructure and rely on spontaneous activity.

A final point to be made is one that has often been stressed by commentators on electronic communications: success depends upon the involvement of a certain critical mass of the target constituency. For many useful purposes, this has to be 100 per cent participation. My impression is that we would not have been able to achieve our own modest levels of involvement had not the computer environment been able to provide considerable supplementary facilities. Thus, many participants are happy to remain active as long as the computer can also furnish, for example, statistical packages for research work, a bibliographic database, access to the library catalogue, JANET access and full screen text processing. It is highly unlikely that electronic mail would have survived in our own case without the attractions of these other facilities.

However, it would be wrong to regard the availability of such facilities as merely sugaring of the communications venture. In our own case, it was intended to exploit the full potential of a shared file space to support and extend undergraduate teaching activity: the potential of database and conferencing packages is particularly relevant in this respect. There is a danger in focusing too exclusively on messaging as the prime electronic resource for enhancing teaching. It might be more properly viewed as just one part of an overall strategy based on distributed computing. This wider conception of the electronic network stresses the place of 'participation' in the life of the department as much as the more familiar (interpersonal) 'communication' theme.

15. Take a balloon and a piece of string

Bridget Somekh and Susan Groundwater-Smith
Cambridge Institute of Education
(Bridget Somekh is now at the University of East Anglia)

Introduction
This paper on work in progress is based on the UK/USA Communications
Project in Cambridgeshire during 1986/87. It is largely drawn from the
Project Report, 'Take A Balloon and a Piece of String', by Bridget Somekh
and Susan Groundwater-Smith presented to the UK/USA Microelectronics
Seminar in Seattle, USA, in May 1987. The full report and a video film are
available from the National Union of Teachers who sponsored the project
together with the National Educational Association in the USA. The work
was carried out with a grant for the purchase of hardware from British
Telecom and with the support of Cambridgeshire LEA and the Cambridgeshire TVEI project. We should like to thank all those who made the project
possible, particularly the teachers and pupils in the eight project schools
and Annette Norman and Charles Worth who provided invaluable support.

The project in Cambridgeshire is part of an international network which
includes two other main geographical areas: Newcastle-upon-Tyne, UK,
where work is led by Michael Clark of West Denton High School; and
Massachussetts, USA, where work is led by Alan November of Wellesley
High School. Two of the Cambridge schools have also established a link
with a kibbutz school in Israel. The aims of the project in all three areas are
broadly similar but some regional differences have developed as the project
has continued, due mainly to the differing interests and backgrounds of the
co-ordinators. The aims of the project in Cambridgeshire are set out below:

a) to explore the effects on young people's writing of communicating by
    electronic mail (E-mail) with a real audience of other young people in
    the UK and the USA;

b) to increase young people's awareness of the role of technology in
    present day society and encourage them to see themselves as active
    users of Information Technology;

c) to increase the awareness of teachers and pupils of their own role as
    members of an international community, made up of people with
    different cultures;

d) to examine ways of helping young people to edit and improve their
    work through word processing, possibly working in collaborative
    groups;

e) to monitor the response of the participating teachers to a major technological innovation and develop understanding of the in-service support needed.

Work is being carried out in five secondary and three primary schools, chosen to give a balance between the north and south of the county and a mix of age range and rural and urban backgrounds:

The Beeches Primary School, 4-11 year-olds, Peterborough
Bretton Woods Community School, 11-18 year-olds, Peterborough
Walton Comprehensive School, 11-18 year-olds, Peterborough
Sawtry Village College, 11-16 year-olds, near Peterborough
Swavesey Village College, 11-16 year-olds, near Cambridge
Parkside Community College, 11-16 year-olds, Cambridge
Milton Road Junior School, 7-11 year-olds, Cambridge
Milton Road Infants School, 4-7 year-olds, Cambridge

The schools all received some financial assistance for the first year but were not fully funded by the project. By a process of negotiation, each school was equipped with a telephone line dedicated to electronic communications, a modem, a year's subscription to The Times Network for Schools (TTNS), BBC B or Master computers, Communitel Infoview viewdata software and word processing facilities (either Wordwise Plus or View).

Note on the technology
TTNS provides schools with an electronic mail and database service for a year at a flat subscription rate, with no further charges for time on the system. Nor is there any charge for filing information on the system, which was very helpful for research purposes. There is an extra charge of £30 for an international mailbox. To this must be added telephone charges, mostly at local call rate. While expense is a major cause of concern for the teachers, this service compares very favourably with what is available in the USA. The small TTNS team have been helpful when asked, both with on-line advice and with occasional visits.

TTNS is not completely trouble free. It is often slow at peak times, such as between 4 and 5pm at the end of afternoon school. The electronic mail service is command driven and there is no easy access to on-line help: it cannot be called user friendly.

The British Telecom telephone service is normally excellent in the Cambridge area because there is access by a local call to a Packet Switch Stream node. In Peterborough, however, schools have to choose between the Epad service which is very slow because of in-built data checking, or a telephone call to the Cambridge node at double the charge. As well as being slow, it is not always easy to make a telephone connection through Epad.

The process of acclimatisation
Planning for the project and acquiring funding to make it possible delayed the start until September 1986. The first major lesson then to be learnt was that everything must go forward much more slowly than we had anticipated. As a result, this report written in April 1987 can only be an account of preliminary work. As such, however, it has a particular value, since there are many lessons to be learnt from analysing the initial stages of such a major innovation.

The Cambridgeshire teachers went through a process of acclimatisation, lasting between three and six months, which we now believe to have been inescapable. During that period, they could see little return for their efforts in terms of educational value to their pupils from the use of E-mail. Consequently, they had to maintain enthusiasm almost as an act of faith. Some of the reasons for this period of acclimatisation are set out below.

The teachers in the project had been deliberately chosen for their interest in word processing and communications, not for their expertise with technology. The project set out to work with teachers of high professional standing who would place educational interests before fascination with the technology for its own sake. We were setting out to test the value of E-mail for education, deliberately avoiding adopting a missionary spirit which might have led to uncritical acceptance of E-mail.

Nevertheless, these teachers were not technologically illiterate. Nearly all of them were already competent users of word processing in their teaching. Yet, E-mail proved to be a major challenge. Adopting its use as part of the curriculum represented a major innovation.

The level of support available to project teachers was not great, there being no full-time project team. It might be regarded as being of the order which a Local Education Authority could afford to provide from its normal resources. Telephone calls and E-mail messages were responded to rapidly and visits sometimes made to a school the following morning. In-service training sessions were arranged for schools as requested. However, there were no regular visits to schools and teachers proved to vary considerably in how much support they asked for. There was a major difficulty in offering support because initially teachers could not be relied on to read their electronic mail and 'phone calls could be misinterpreted as 'interrogatory check-ups' rather than offers of help.

Group meetings proved to be invaluable but attending them was a further call on time in a project which already made big demands on teachers' time.

The teachers' difficulties fell into a number of categories:

a)   technical difficulties, both with TTNS itself and with spooling word processed files ready for transmission or downloading files to disk for printing or editing;

b)   practical difficulties to do with the availability of equipment for easy use, including the positioning of the telephone line and problems with being unable to leave the modem permanently connected;

c)   personal difficulties to do with poor self-image in relation to technology, making for anxiety and tension;

d)   institutional difficulties to do with inflexibilities in the system, such as with time-tabling of micro use (so that pupils could only spend a very short time word processing each week) and with security (necessitating carrying heavy equipment up and down stairs);

e)   anxieties over costs, making people hesitant to use the system for more than a few minutes: this was particularly limiting in the early stages when the only way of gaining confidence with the system was to spend time on-line; once the first bills had come in and proved to be reasonable, everyone was able to be more relaxed;

f)   shortage of teacher time in a very full programme of work, making it impossible to establish a regular pattern of going on-line every day; and making attendance at after-school meetings difficult (these meetings which were intended to be supportive also constituted an extra burden of work);

g)   the absence of established personal and work routines for E-mail, so that it could not be slipped into an odd five minutes, and using it never saved time.

Choices about the nature and purpose of electronic mail communication
E-mail is used in the business world in two ways:

a)   for on-line writing of short messages;
b)   for the transfer of word processed documents.

The Cambridgeshire project decided to focus on word processing for two reasons:

a)   it cut down on-line time, reducing telephone costs;
b)   it encouraged the use of word processing with all the advantages its editing facilities offer in the teaching of writing.

This decision fitted with the project's aims in Cambridgeshire as outlined above. Much of the project's work has focused on the ways in which word processing supports the teaching of writing. In addition, the E-mail project has acted as an incentive for teachers of English and languages to use word processing. As one teacher of computer applications said, 'There's much more word processing going on this term than there ever would have been without electronic mail.'

The decision to focus on transmitting word processed texts had important implications, however, because it meant that pupils were not experiencing the new mode of communication which is specific to E-mail, with its informality, its immediacy, its free use of abbreviations and its tolerance of typing errors. It was a decision which was natural to the Cambridgeshire teachers whose background was in English and language teaching but it might be open to question by those with a background in computer applications, particularly by American colleagues who are used to a telephone system which makes no charges for local calls.

On-line writing also takes place, mainly but not exclusively, between teachers or between them and Bridget Somekh. It has become increasingly important as a source of mutual support and its convenience has become a strong motivating force for teachers as they have begun to feel comfortable with the system. With hindsight, it is clear that, from the start, more emphasis should have been put on this form of communication between participating teachers. Anxieties over costs proved to be relatively groundless and some of the major difficulties experienced in the first term, particularly and ironically with regard to slowness of response to E-mailed word processed texts, would have been at least partly overcome in this way.

Building communication into the curriculum
E-mail is for the purpose of communication. Before considering its use by pupils in the project, it is worth remembering that schools do not make full educational use of some other conventional forms of communication, such as the postal service and the telephone. Children make telephone calls at home and they probably write letters occasionally, but at school they are only likely to use these forms of communication in simulated circumstances. It is precisely because schools are concerned to open curriculum links with the world outside that E-mail offers an attractive opportunity. However, the school curriculum does not offer ready-made structures to facilitate its use. One of the biggest challenges of the project has always been, 'What should the pupils write?' Inherently, this is not a problem of E-mail, it is a problem relating to the basic structure and assumptions of the educational curriculum. In schools, pupils normally write for their teachers or for each other. Moreover, although they may

publish their work in some form, such as in magazines or simply posted up on the classroom wall, they do not *interact* with the audiences for this writing. Normally, teachers and pupils communicate with each other (by writing and talking) within enclosed classrooms, unless teachers plan for a special activity.

From the beginning, it was decided to use E-mail within the curriculum, to enhance work with a clear educational purpose. Initial ideas included:

a)   collaborative story writing over a distance: with groups of thirteen year-olds in three secondary schools writing first instalments to be passed on to groups in the other schools for 'middles' and 'endings'; and with nine year-old primary school pupils sending out story beginnings to be finished by others;

b)   communications between a mysterious Mary Tudor (played by secondary pupils) and ten year-old primary school pupils engaged in the 'Mary Rose' computer simulation project;

c)   a link between thirteen year-olds in Cambridge reading a book called 'The Machine Gunners' set in Newcastle and pupils in Newcastle able to provide local information to set the book in a more meaningful context;

d)   communications between mysterious travellers from Jupiter (played first by nine year-olds but eventually by an adult) and seven year-old children working on a project on 'The Planets';

e)   communications between fifteen year-old pupils studying 'Animal Farm' and others with similar interests, sharing ideas on Utopian Societies, real or imaginary (this was an idea which was never put into practice);

f)   communications between nine year-old pupils in Cambridge and children in a kibbutz school in Israel, aiming to share information about their school and their lives to promote awareness of cultural differences and build mutual understanding. (This went ahead by the exchange of writing both by hand and through conventional post but an electronic mail link was not achieved.)

It soon became clear that to use E-mail in this way required teachers to engage in joint lesson planning of a quite detailed kind. Locally, it has been possible to arrange regular meetings and, in theory, E-mail itself provides a strong communication link. In practice, even on a local basis, this kind of dovetailing of educational purposes is complex and problematic. Further afield, E-mail has been depended on as the only link and it has proved ineffective in enabling the necessary creative interaction, though it is unclear whether this will remain so once the use of E-mail is well established and teachers are in the habit of going on-line daily for frequent communication.

Problems during the early stages of the project included:

a) extended time lapses after sending writing before any communication came back, during which time there was no way of knowing whether the other school was working away painstakingly at typing up a response, or had simply not received the mail;

b) assumptions, often disappointed, that the other teacher would respond appropriately because of a shared professionalism: 'I just assumed that he would understand my aims for the writing when he saw the children's work but when the replies came back they were nothing . . . I was so disappointed';

c) unpredictability of pupils' response to the writing received, sometimes lively but sometimes bored, leading to selective replies to only some of the contributions, particularly since the receiving teacher owed commitment to her/his own students but had no natural responsibility to the pupils sending out the writing.

In effect, successful use of E-mail, fully integrated into the curriculum for two classes in different schools, necessitates team-teaching over a distance. Even locally, with regular meetings, it was impossible to overcome completely the problems involved. Part of the reason lies in the very process of teaching and learning. Before asking pupils to write or read, a teacher sets the scene, gives ideas, arouses enthusiasm. Motivation is vital to learning and therefore teachers are involved in a process of negotiating with their pupils the work to be done. E-mail from another school drops into the classroom without being part of the negotiated context which motivates both pupils and teacher. Only very careful planning, akin to team teaching, can enable both teachers to negotiate compatible contexts.

Learning from experience: freeing up communications
a) Penpal letters
Although the project teachers have never lost their central aim to integrate the use of E-mail into the curriculum, it was clear by Christmas time that the strain of planning all the communications, as outlined above, was too great. At the worst extreme it could take five weeks for writing to come back in response to work that had taken three weeks to type in the first place. Everything was becoming too serious and laborious. It was decided to experiment with a different type of writing: penpal letters from pupils in one school to those in another. Some of these were between children of the same age and sex, but not all. In many cases, they were written by a group of pupils and might be answered by an individual or a group. Often, they

were written in a single session at the computer. There was an art in writing these letters to catch the attention of potential respondees. The biggest problem was that not all received a response. However, some real contacts were made and there was a new sense of excitement for the pupils involved, though this may have partly related to beginning to write to young people in Newcastle and America for the first time.

Some of the most powerful educational messages have come from the cultural differences emerging from these penpal letters. For example, Jennifer, an American High School girl of eighteen, wrote to Khaleda, a nine year-old Pakistani Muslim girl in Peterborough, 'You have a very big family. The clothes you wear sound very interesting. Here we wear almost anything we want. . . . Your religion seems to be a great part of your life, do you agree?' Comparisons could also be made between American and British teenage slang; and pupils enjoyed finding out about differences in free-time activities (involving, amongst other things, a comparison of the licensing laws for alcohol in the USA and the UK). One of the most successful letters of all was a mildly scurrilous piece from fifteen year-olds in Peterborough commenting freely on the way Thatcher and Reagan were presented in the current UK television hit, 'Spitting Image': it struck a sympathetic chord with the students in Massachusetts.

b) Two levels of response
A very simple expedient which was adopted from Christmas onwards has been to think in terms of two levels of response to each communication: a quick immediate reply acknowledging that the writing has been received, giving some indication of the response to be expected; and a full response in whatever time it takes to write it. Although this may seem obvious, it was not what happened naturally. Adopting it as a rule took away a lot of the guilt people began feeling when they found they could not organise responses as quickly as they had hoped. It also did a lot to prevent disappointment when the full answer took a long time to come.

c) Using adults to communicate with children
From the start, there were problems in getting immediate responses back to children's writing. The main difficulty was connected with the slowness with which pupils keyed in text. This was a particular problem for infants and junior age children engaged in projects involving communicating with a fantasy person. In the end, it was clear that adults can provide the required response much more quickly and easily than other children, fitting in more readily with the teacher's aims for the project work. The task is not too onerous since only one letter is required at a time. A particularly splendid piece of fun was Dracula's letter to a secondary English class engaged in reading the book of that name:

'My pet rat is sitting on my lap, cleaning his whiskers, with his little red eyes glowing. . . . My mug of warm blood sits beside me, and I'm just waiting for a jangling on me door-bell so that I can have me next meal . . . SO . . . I must get my wings flexed — I can't hang around here — I must fly! . . .'

d) Seeing E-mail as just one kind of communication to be used in conjunction with all the others

E-mail does not replace other forms of communication: it simply provides different opportunities. No one would dream of giving up visiting friends because face-to-face meetings could be replaced by using the telephone. They cannot. In the same way, using E-mail does not replace the need for teachers to telephone each other occasionally to discuss how things are going. In our project schools where E-mail is being used most successfully, it is often alongside the exchange of photographs, handwritten letters and glossy printed brochures, by means of ordinary post. Some of our most successful communication has been between Milton Road Junior School and Israel where postal links have established a rapport which we hope to extend when we set up the E-mail link in the near future.

Learning from experience: children in control of technology

It was an aim of the project to give young people the experience of being in control of technology, yet, at first, it was impossible to carry this out. These were the reasons:

1. The teachers had to learn to use electronic mail themselves first.

2. There was only one modem in each school so it seemed invidiuous to select some pupils for a special experience denied to the others.

3. Teachers were anxious about the costs of using E-mail and it was assumed that if pupils had access to the password for the system they would run up huge telephone bills.

There have been many ways in which the shortage of resources in UK schools has reaped interesting results for educational computing, not least through the growth of interest in collaborative word processing in groups. Here is another case in point. By Christmas, it was clear that teachers could not cope with the administrative burden of going on-line every day, spooling word processed files and sending them off, downloading incoming files or printing them out. Although this problem has never been wholly solved, it has been greatly eased by entrusting the technology to pupils and using them as willing workers to carry out these administrative tasks. They are well able to do it, as we discovered when one group of ten year-olds, to whom the password had *not* been entrusted, worked out what it was by watching their teacher's fingers on the keyboard and went on-line without him, to change it for a joke! From Christmas onwards, significantly, after the arrival of the first telephone bills, most of the teachers have entrusted the password to a small group of children and let them take over some of the very real burden of work. This has proved to be entirely successful, as the password can always be changed by the teacher to remove the privilege if it is abused (to our knowledge it never has been).

By April, when our American colleague visited one primary school, a group of ten year-olds with no teacher present was able to set up the computer, find the disk and load the software, enter TTNS and help him to send a message to America (though they had to be told the American mailbox number which involves paying an extra international charge).

The human interface with technology
Technology is only useful if it serves people, but people need to adapt to new rituals to use technology easily. This they find difficult to do, although once acquired the new rituals can be just as friendly and reassuring as the old ones. Bridget Somekh writes: by way of example, I can explain that when I first used a word processor I was lost without the feel of the pen in my hand and the familiar positioning of the pad of paper and coffee mug on my desk: now my keyboard has a comforting familiarity and the mat for my coffee mug waits on the monitor stand. It is the same with E-mail. When I get back to the office in the evening nowadays, I am used to going on-line to find out who has sent me a message: it is the very same feeling I always get when lifting my mail off the doormat. Because E-mail is now fitted into my daily rituals, it is quick and convenient for me to check my mailbox. But this did not happen all at once. First, I had to go through a period when the process was slow, confusing and inconvenient.

Throughout the project, it has become clear that most of the technical problems have been caused by this human interface with technology. There have been many such problems and they have been very frustrating. Understanding them is the key to understanding why there has to be that 3-6 month period of acclimatisation experienced by the Cambridgeshire teachers, as described at the beginning of this paper.

Much of the problem is in having to rely on other people for information and expertise. We have discovered that experts hate to say that something is impossible. If they think there is a chance they could do something if they worked at it for two days, they will say it can be done: but, of course, when it comes to actually doing it, they are very unlikely to have the time to spare. On the other hand, the field of technology is changing so fast that they may say that something is possible because they believe it will be in six months' time.

Another problem specific to using E-mail is in having to rely on other people to organise things which are more your priority than theirs. This can make you quite unreasonable. On the other hand, people who are not experts in technology can easily underestimate the difficulty they will have in doing something. You need to be very patient and understanding when it becomes clear that someone is not able to sort out the technology at their end — when all the time you have been thinking that once your own problems were sorted out everything would fall into place.

One of the main problems is that the world of education simply does not have the money to command the world of technology. Many of our difficulties in setting up E-mail links between the UK and the USA have been caused by differences in the telephone systems between the two countries. This leads to technical problems in transmitting data communications between the two systems. By chance, it would have been much easier for us to communicate with Australian teachers — but this was not our project! Currently, there are two or three large international E-mail systems which cannot communicate with each other: the British Telecom/ Dialcom system (easily compatible with the UK telephone system) is one, and the Western Union/Easilink system (easily compatible with the USA telephone system) is another. I am led to believe that it would not be impossible to link the two but it is not in the commercial interests of either to do so.

Finally, there is no underestimating the problems caused when human error comes into contact with the total inflexibility of computer technology. In a few years' time, the software will be friendlier. With a more expensive system, things would probably be much easier now. Nevertheless, leaving out a single figure in our American colleague's mailbox number set the UK/ USA link back by a whole month; and our colleague at the Hebrew University of Jerusalem sent us a number of messages on JANET (Joint Academic Network) which never arrived because he was making a small error in typing in a fifteen character sequence of letters and symbols.

One can do little about all this other than record it. We are tempted to say that nothing can be more frustrating and more fascinating than the way in which human beings interface with technology.

Plans for continuing work
The project teachers in Cambridgeshire now form an established support group experienced in using E-mail with their pupils. Work will continue, as planned, focusing on the following areas:

a) on-line communication between teachers;

b)   cross-curricular work, drawing in more teachers from the project schools;

c)   planned, integrated projects between schools, which will be easier to organise with the experience and greater confidence gained from the first two terms' work;

d)   development of databases of information using Communitel Infoview, linking to the Cambridgeshire host in Peterborough;

e)   further development of the links with Newcastle, Massachusetts and Israel as more schools join the network;

f)   development of confidence in more pupils with on-line communication, checking the mailbox and handling word processed files.

Summary of the main findings from the preliminary work of the project
Logistic points

1.   There is likely to be a period of acclimatisation with the technology, lasting between three and six months. During this time, teachers will be overcoming a range of problems which involve establishing personal rituals to make the use of E-mail convenient. This is a time of positive learning and cannot be avoided or hurried. In-service support is very important during this stage when teachers may see little educational value in using E-mail.

2.   A decision will need to be made as to whether to concentrate on transmitting word processed files or developing pupils' use of on-line communications. Both are valid but offer very different educational experiences.

3.   On-line communication between teachers is essential to back up any exchange of word processed files. If possible, teachers need to go on-line every day to check the mailbox (see 4 below).

4.   Pupils themselves should be given direct access to E-mail (possibly working as a small group with a special duty), including entrusting them with the mailbox password: in this way, teachers are not burdened with a secretarial role of sending files and printing mail, and pupils gain a real sense of the power of technology (passwords can easily be changed in the rare cases when pupils abuse their privilege).

5.   E-mail does not replace other forms of communication: it simply provides different opportunities. It is most effective when used alongside other communications such as letter writing and the exchanging of photographs and parcels; and, where possible, the telephone and face-to-face meetings.

Educational points

6. Communicating interactively with groups or individuals outside the classroom is not an established part of the school curriculum. This gives rise to a major problem expressed in the key question, 'What should the pupils write?' One of the strengths of E-mail is that it provides opportunities for opening up classrooms to outside contacts but, without natural communication structures, teachers have to plan carefully.

7. Despite 6 above, E-mail is of most value when it is used with a real curriculum purpose. However, this necessitates careful planning, akin to team teaching over a distance. Frequent contact between the teachers involved is essential, whether by on-line communication or by other means.

8. Despite 7 above, it is important that the writing does not become too serious. It is important to give pupils the opportunity of getting to know each other through exchanging penpal letters and questions. Some of the most powerful educational messages come from the cultural differences emerging from penpal letters.

9. The time taken between sending off a batch of word processed files and receiving replies can become a major problem. One practical suggestion for coping with this is to send two levels of response, the first a one-line response immediately on receiving the mail, the second a full word processed response when it is ready. A second practical suggestion is to use adults sometimes to reply to students' letters.

Suggestions for supporting teachers using electronic mail

It is clear that in-service support is essential for teachers beginning to use E-mail. Our experience suggests the following:

a) a support group of teachers in other local schools who come together for regular meetings to plan interactive work; as the group gains in confidence, members will increase the amount of support they give each other on-line;

b) a co-ordinator (LEA advisory teacher, seconded teacher, lecturer from a local college), with an understanding of the threatening nature of a major innovation for the participants, who can maintain contacts, provide technical support and monitor progress; again, this support will come more and more on-line;

c) a small amount of financial backing from the LEA and/or an outside sponsor, to pay for dedicated telephone lines and necessary hardware;

d)   technical support from someone in the institution (or able to visit at short notice); if possible, this should be from someone who understands how to share problems rather than demonstrating her/his own expertise;

e)   moral support from colleagues within the school, sharing problems and passing on newly acquired knowledge.

The Cambridge case studies

While the world of commerce has learned to use the modem with some security and sophistication, for schools the technology is still very much of the 'Toy Town' variety; simple, partially effective but liable to breakdown. The situation is reminiscent of the early hands-on stage of mass media education when teachers and learners in classrooms attempted epic productions with Super 8 cameras, exhilarating and frustrating at one and the same time. This is not, however, to decry the complexity of the *educational* experience but to argue that the experience itself is embedded within a pioneering framework, with all of the uncertainty and risk-taking that that entails.

The two teachers with whom we worked, Pat and Andrew, were both experienced in their work; Pat as a teacher of mixed ability nine to ten year-olds in a culturally homogeneous (as far as that is possible) Cambridge primary school and Andrew as faculty head in the English Department of a Comprehensive secondary school, which catered for a socially more diverse group, also in Cambridge. As well, they could both be described as relatively recent users of microcomputers, having been stimulated by the schools' purchases of the technology, rather than as 'hackers' of some experience.

Pat: 'Well, initially, it's the awful story you know, the school bought the computers and didn't know what to do with them and nobody used them. We had several programs in the early stages which were full of games, just treated as games really, I think pretty well all the staff felt we weren't getting much out of it. . . . When I found out about the word processing part, which I liked, or have worked on most . . . that's when I became interested. I suppose it's probably over a year that I've been using it, using it constructively.'

As well as enthusiasm, both have a healthy scepticism regarding the 'gee whiz' nature of the technology.

Andrew: 'It's just one of many media. . . . But because the computers are in a separate room, one has to actually find pretexts for using them . . . one has to organise one's ways into using them.'

The 'organising into' use of the computers was further stimulated in this instance by the introduction of the modem. The proposal was to:

'Set up electronic mail and amateur satellite links between three regional networks in the UK and three similar networks in the USA. . . . We wanted to look at the effect on children's writing of having a real audience of other children. Some of whom would come from very different backgrounds; we also wanted to give children control of the technology now in common use for communications in the world of business and industry.' (Somekh, 1986, p17.)

The result of this aspiration was, as has already been indicated in the first part of this report, to install modems in schools in Cambridge, Peterborough and Newcastle and to form social professional networks between the users in such ways that the teachers would determine the actual curriculum. Similar networks were established in the United States. Several mini-projects ensued, among them a writing link with Israel, cultural correspondence, a progressive story writing activity, and exchange in the US schools in Massachusetts. An additional writing project was initiated at the Cambridge comprehensive school by the postgraduate teacher education student.

Organising into using the modem
It was Pat who took up the challenge of establishing a link with a kibbutz in Israel. Her initial interest grew rather less from the technology and more from a concern to have a vehicle for carrying forward her desire to teach children the principles of anti-racism.

She believed that this was best done, not by instructing the children in anti-racism, by giving them a set of propositions or edicts by which they should live, but by handling and understanding information in such a manner that the children would think in moral ways.

Pat was concerned to make moral thinking more explicit (eg Hirst, 1974 pp 132-151). She attempted to do this within the framework of a major project for one term, ie 'Israel'. Much time was spent by children doing their own research in small groups on such background information as history, geography and wildlife.

Pat: 'I really was uncertain about how it would turn out. I hoped the children would be able to sort of . . . not just learn from books. You know you can do that, in the old fashioned way, just "learn" a country. But I hoped the children would be able to ask more probing questions of other children, a sort of cultural exchange really.'

Certainly, this involved a study of books but it also required the children to project themselves in various ways into the experience of others. What was it like to experience persecutions, dislocation, disenfranchisement, the birth of a nation and the subsequent life of that country? The background was achieved via discussing, for example, *The Diary of Anne Frank*, via a study of the Old Testament and via the telling of myths and legends. Parents who were Jewish were of assistance here as they came to the school and re-told the classical Jewish stories. But the lynch pin was to be the electronic mail exchange with the children of the kibbutz.

Andrew took up two challenges. With his year 3 class of thirteen and fourteen year-olds, the writing-by-instalment work has been undertaken with text being received from Peterborough built upon by the Cambridge children and then sent on to a third school. Also, contact was made by the year 4 class with their American counterparts. Alongside Andrew there worked Ian, a postgraduate teacher education student. He had chosen, as a major project, to study intensively Robert Westall's *The Machine Gunners* (1975) with a year 2 class. Since the novel is set in Newcastle, it was Ian's intention that the children use the Newcastle link to elaborate and enrich their consciousness of the context in which the book was set.

Apart from the obvious differences between the organisation of primary and secondary schools, there was a second difference in the ways in which Pat, Andrew and Ian organised themselves into using the microcomputer and the modem. In Pat's case, the school owns two microcomputers. Although these machines do have a designated location, they are on trolleys and easily moved about the school. In most instances, when we saw them in use, the computers were actually in the classroom. By way of contrast, the computers at the comprehensive school are in a room specifically assigned for that purpose. (In neither instance is ergonomically-designed furniture available.) In both cases, there was an emphasis upon the computers being used by groups of children rather than by individuals. This meant, then, that the act of writing texts to be sent hither and yon was a public, collaborative act and hence somewhat different in nature from the private, personal writing that most school children engage in. (Private here is being used in the sense that it is hidden between the pages of an individual student's book written only for the teachers' eye, other than the occasional piece which is 'published' in one form or another.)

Writing for an unknown audience carries with it significant responsibility to 'get it right'. The capacity of word processing as a tool for sustained editing has been remarked upon by many concerned and interested in children's writing (Clark, 1985, Sandery, 1986, Somekh, 1986). Within the project, much has been dependent upon sufficient time being made available for such editing to occur. Andrew, on several occasions, regretted the fragmentary organisation of secondary schooling which mitigated against careful, negotiated editing. While Nancy Martin (1983) reminds us that those managerial constraints are not immutable, the actuality is that there is great rigidity in this schooling sector. Pat's groups were much more manoeuvrable, both in time and space. The temporal features of the project were present in other manifestations also. A significant question became 'How does one sustain the energies over a considerable period of time, given the vagaries and uncertainties of the technology?' The modem link with Israel has been difficult to establish so that word processed material has ultimately been sent by conventional mail.

Pat: 'I was disappointed (in the link not being established) in that I felt I had actually put a lot of effort into it and the children had spent about five weeks solidly really working to get enough stuff to send, and presenting it as well as they could. They'd really stayed in at lunchtimes and got really keyed up and excited, so it was a disappointment to them and me.'

Altogether, Pat had given four months to the project and now thought the time had come judiciously to withdraw (although another teacher in the school has proposed to continue the project as a club activity).

Andrew continues to see benefits in continuing the project but is frustrated by technological difficulties. Following the British Telecom dispute, there was a problem in being re-assigned a call sign.

Andrew: 'The project is at times uneven, patchy. It's hard to organise some sort of pacing, the sending, waiting, receiving, the only pattern is an uneven one. At times one doesn't even know if the stuff has been delivered. It would be different if you just had a computer there all the time on your desk top.'

Given these frustrations and difficulties and acknowledging the complexities of the students' experiences, how can we best justify the project?

What is the worthwhileness of a project such as this?
Lawrence Stenhouse once wrote:

'If we are to reinterpret humanism, then we must look towards a vernacular humanism, which through the use of languages, domestically familiar to him, opens to the students a ready access to knowledge. . . . An educational programme which would make realistic this aspiration is difficult to mount even under the most favourable conditions. It involves the formidable problem of expressing knowledge in those forms and activities which both invite and strengthen the judgements of the learner.' (Stenhouse, 1983, p 166.)

What Stenhouse is so eloquently reminding us of is the need for schooling to provide conditions which will allow learners not only to exercise judgements but also to allow engagements with that judgement. Defence and counter-defence need to be mounted with students learning to construct and conduct arguments regarding the nature of knowledge itself.

It is precisely in the matter of judgement that the project's strength lies. Not the judgement of teachers but the judgements of learners themselves. Take the way that the learners make language work for them in the following incident.

Pat had invited into her class a Jewish mother to tell of the festival of Purim. So animated were the children by the presentation, that they set about making a series of masks representing the characters in the ancient story.

The masks themselves were well made and took quite some time. The children decided to display them in the school foyer with an accompanying explanation of the characters' roles and their relationship one with the other and the unfolding events. A small group gathered around the computer telling and re-telling the story.

One of them, Melody, was concerned about tying the characters together. At the behest of David and Deborah, she had entered 'Mordichai was an old and wise Jewish man. He had a niece called Esther.' On her own initiative she added '(You will read about her below.)' David protested.

David: 'This is starting to sound like a magazine story.' (Parodying Melody) 'You will read about her below.'

Melody: 'No need to be nasty. It's to organise — to see. They now know what will be coming.'

Deborah: 'That's fair, David. Melody's right. Now we have to write about bowing to Haman.'

David: 'Alright — how about "Mordichai did not think he should bow down . . .?"' (Melody typed this in.)

Deborah: 'Stop! What do you mean "think"? He *knew* he shouldn't bow — it was the law.'

David: 'It's the same thing.'

Deborah: 'No it isn't. Thinking means you've got choices. I think I'll watch football. . . . I think I'll go to the markets. . . . Mordichai had no choices. He *knew* because it was *the law*.'

David: 'I see. But if we say all that, it will be too hard for people reading it. What about . . . what about . . .'

Melody *(having deleted the last sentence):* 'Just keep it simple "Mordichai did not bow to Haman".'

David: 'But we should mention the law.'

Deborah: 'Take out the full stop and say something like "because of his religion".'

David: 'His Jewish religion.'

Melody: 'That's it, that's right now.'

WHY WE MADE THE MASKS
We made these masks because of the Jewish festival called Purim. It is celebrated in the springtime. People often make carnival masks. There are several characters in the story of Purim.

AHASHVEROSH
One of them is Ahashverosh he was the king of Shushan where the story is based. He was a very foolish king because he always did what his advisors told him to.

HAMAN
Haman was an advisor to the king and he was a very evil man. He thought that he was so powerful that everyone should bow down to him. Mordichai the Jew would not bow to him, this made Haman very angry and he decided to ask the king if he could kill all Jews. The king was not really concentrating so he said yes.

MORDICHAI
Mordichai was an old and wise Jewish man. He had a niece called Esther. (You will read about her below.) Mordichai did not bow to Haman because of this Jewish religion.

ESTHER
Esther was a very beautiful woman and she married the king Ahashverosh because she won a beauty contest. So, she became Queen of Shushan. When she heard about Haman's evil plot she was very upset because she was a Jew. She plucked up enough courage to ask the king if the law could be reversed. The king agreed to this but it was too late to be undone. So the king put up a notice to say all the Jews could fight for their lives.

This exchange, at first sight a relatively simple one, is indeed the crafting of information into knowledge. Nine year-old children are here examining a profound philosophical question: 'What is the difference between conjecture and absolute authority?' The exchanges, the modifications are not merely surface editing, they are the result of children making their own judgements, making language work for them. Halliday (1985) in the conclusion to his linguistic text *Spoken and Written Language* points out that, as new demands are made of language, so language changes in response to them (p82). This project, in its own modest way, is making new demands upon the 'language games' of young learners and, as such, may indeed be judged to be educationally worthwhile. Adams (1985) has personified the computer as a kind of:

> 'Neutral, non-threatening and non-censorious, silent chair of a group, which provides a focus for activity, keeps the group motivated, responds to whatever the group does, but also leaves its members free to make their own decisions. . . .' (Adams, 1985, p43.)

He goes on to claim that, as yet, we do not know a great deal about the effects of collaborative writing or the sort of talk generated by the process. Another kind of worthwhileness which this project has achieved has been to give teachers tangible evidence that the process and the product are two sides of the one coin, with the currency being children's thinking — a currency of immense value.

In conclusion
These statements about worthwhileness should not, however, be read as an uncritical testimonial for the project. Its awkward attenuated nature makes it a difficult one to manage. Electronic mail between schools is in its infancy. We have, here, merely pulled up a few radishes to see whether they are growing. They will need much nuturing and tending if they are to come to full fruition.

References
Adams, A (1985), Talking, Listening and the Microcomputer, in Chandler, D and Marcus, S (eds), *Computers and Literacy*, Open University Press, Milton Keynes, pp41-55.

Bruley, K (1985), *TTNS Getting Started (for schools)*, MEP Southern Region Microelectronics Information Centre.

Clark, D (1985), Young Writers and the Computer, in Chandler, D and Marcus, S (eds), *Computers and Literacy*, Ibid, pp12-25.

Derbyshire (1985) — *Introducing Electronic Mail* is available from Mr Steve Sansom, Advisory Teacher for Computer Education, Chatsworth Hall, Matlock, Derbyshire DE4 3FW.

Derbyshire (1985) — a report of the Merlin Project is available from the Headmaster, Mr C Butler, Chaddesdon Park Junior School, Tennisee Road, Chaddesdon, Derbyshire.

Devonshire — further information about the DATEM project is available from Mr John Ralston, Adviser for Computers in Education, County Hall, Exeter EX2 4QG.

Halliday, M (1985), *Spoken and Written Language,* Deakin University Press, Geelong.

Hirst, P (1974), *Knowledge and the Curriculum*, Routledge and Kegan Paul, London.

Martin, N (1983), Contests Are More Important Than We Know, in Arnold, R (ed), *Timely Voices: English Teaching in the Eighties,* Oxford University Press, Melbourne.

Sandery, P (1986), Computers and Writing, in Nilander, J (ed), *The Teacher's Story: The IBM Secondary Schools Education Project*, The IBM Corporation, Sydney.

Smith, R (1987), *At the Crossroads of New Methods, Old Problems and New Technologies,* paper given at the International Conference on Oracy, University of East Anglia, April.

Somekh, B (1986), *Exploring Word Processing with Children,* paper presented to the Symposium 'Applications of Word Processing in the Classroom' held at NFER, October.

Somekh, B and Groundwater-Smith, S (1987), *Take a Balloon and a Piece of String: Report of the UK/USA Communications Project,* paper presented to UK/USA micro-electronics seminar, Seattle, USA, May (available from National Union of Teachers).

Stenhouse, L (1983), *Authority, Education and Emancipation,* Heinemann Educational, London.

16. Group communications via computer conferencing — the educational potential

David McConnell
University of Bath

Introduction

Computer mediated communications (CMC) offer the potential of linking together learners and researchers in institutions at all levels of the educational sector.

In this paper, I will consider the possibilities of CMC as a method of group communications within formal education. I will describe one particular use of the CoSy computer conferencing system in conducting educational seminars — and will present some preliminary research outcomes into group interactions and discussions using the medium — and will conclude by considering the potential of computer conferencing within educational action research, INSET and distance learning.

Group communications via computer mediated communications

Computer mediated communications allow for a variety of types of communications, each of which can be used for *group* correspondence. Existing facilities include electronic mail, bulletin boards and computer conferencing.

Electronic mail
Conventional electronic mail primarily supports communication between individuals. Users can send and receive personal messages, which are logged by the system. Some software allows users to reply to messages with attached copies of the original message sent back to the originator, thus allowing the path of the correspondence to be displayed. For example, Figure 16.1 shows a series of electronic mail messages sent between two individuals on the CoSy computer conferencing system.

In addition, group communications are possible by the use of distribution lists which allow the same message to be sent to large groups. But this becomes a cumbersome method of group correspondence if used constantly. Nevertheless, the combination of a 'reply' facility and distribution lists does permit some limited form of group communications in ordinary E-mail systems.

Bulletin boards
Bulletin boards (bboards) take group communications one step further by allowing any user to 'pin' messages on to a communal message space so

```
Mail :1784
Memo #1784
From: mikes
Date: 24-FEB-1987 09:51:47.
To: dmc
Message-Id:  <memo.1784>
In-Reply-To:  <memo.1780>
Subject: Dissertation
I am in a video meet from 1130 approx .Is 1030 or 1045 poss?
If not is later in the day possible eg 1430?
Thanks Mike

-------- Original Message --------

Yes we can meet on Tuesday, but I'm booked at 1100.
How about 1200?
David

-------- Original Message --------

I have worked out the questions I wish to ask on my first
structured interviews.Can we meet Tue 24 at 1100 to discuss?
```

Figure 16.1 — Electronic mail messages

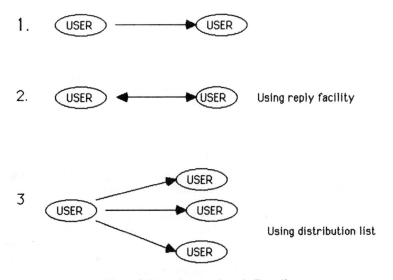

Figure 16.2 — Interaction via E-mail

that all users can read them. Any correspondence between the group can take place via the bboard so that everyone can share in the communications.

Although many bboards allow users to manipulate the entries, for example by searching message headers and text for keywords, a bboard is essentially only a method of display and is not structured for high levels of *interactive* group communications. An example of the structure and layout of messages on a bulletin board is given in Figure 16.3.

Computer conferencing (CC)
Computer conferencing (CC) allows for communal *interactive* group communications. Messages are typed on to a communal message space but users can attach new messages to existing ones in a way that allows a conversation to develop.

Overview of CoSy
The CoSy computer conferencing system is structured for group com-munications. The system supports conventional personal electronic mail; conferences for communications between large groups of people; and conversations for small group correspondence. (See Fig 16.4, page 150.)

On accessing CoSy, a user is informed of their mail and conference status and the conferences which have new messages in them, ie messages which have been added since their last log-in. They can also request a list of all available conferences. (See Fig 16.5, page 151.)

Each conference is a computer record of an on-going discussion which any user can join and participate in at any time. Participants can enter 'free-standing' unassociated messages when they wish to say something new, or when they wish to start a new thread of discourse within the general discussion. They can also comment on a message entered by someone else. Their comment is 'attached' to the one they are commenting on. This is indicated in the message header where readers are alerted to the fact that the message is a comment on a previous one. In this way, using special commands in the conferencing software, users can follow a conversation from the initial message through all associated messages without having to read any unassociated messages within the same conference.

A computer conference may last days, weeks or even months. Any user can easily set up a conference; no knowledge of computing is needed. Each conference is overseen by a *moderator*, usually the person who established the conference. The role of the moderator is to start the conference off and ensure that it follows its defined purpose. The moderator has certain 'privileged' controls over the conference, eg s/he can delete messages (for

```
Mail-Manager>read 60:62
 Message 60 (766 characters):
Sender: PMT600.AW-BOEHM
Date:  7 Apr 1987 2102-GMT
From: _BOEHM ILFORD <PMT600.AW-BOEHM at KL2183>
Subject: Industrial application of UCSD Pascal, Pascal
To: PMT600

Dear colleages,
I would like to hear from anybody who is using Pascal
in an industrial enviroment i.e. process control or
CAD/CAM  ec.
I work in the field of advanced manufacturing and
specialise in the  of image analysis, for
robotics and the semiconductor manufacturer.

My present hardware set-up is:
Zoom macroscope 400x magn. ,
SONY bw slow scan camera,
Framegrabber 10 bit ,
Kemitron computer Z 80 based operating system.
If anybody would like to contact me, please
leave a message cn the BBOARD  my code:
PMT600.AW-BOEHM  thank you.
Alphonse BOEHM
-------
   ========
Read>
 Message 61 (493 characters):
Sender: PMT600.JM-EMMS
Date:  6 May 1987 1433-GMT
From: J.M. Emms - Milton Keynes <PMT600.JM-EMMS at KL2183>
Subject: ring buffer overflow
To: pmt600
cc: pmt600.jm-emms

If anyone else has problems with ring buffer overflow please put a message
on the bboard so that I can make my comments more generally available.
Using an electronic mail system means we all need to change our working
practices slightly, I replied to the individual rather than the board!
-------
   ========
Read>
 Message 62 (396 characters):
Sender: PMT600.DJ-LEWIS
Date:  7 May 1987 2022-GMT
From: D.J. Lewis - Cardiff <PMT600.DJ-LEWIS at KL2183>
Subject: SAQ 4.4 Unit 7
To: PMT600

   Is it just me or does anyone else get a slightly different answer to this one
?  Shouldn't the WHILE symbols be in bon their own if you apply the rules as lay
ed down in the preceeding ?
                 Any comments.......
-------
   ========
```

Fig 16.3 — Structure and layout of messages on a bulletin board (from Open University bboard for pmt600, Software Engineering Course. See Emms and McConnell, 1987)

The CoSy conferencing system is made up of several sub-systems :

CONFERENCES

Conferences are electronic meeting places. Conferences may be open to everyone or only to invited participants. Most conferences usually have more than one topic, arranged round a theme. For example, a conference on DOGS could have topics on BREEDING; TRAINING; TYPES; HEALTH, and so on.

It is within these topics that participants read what is being said, and enter 'messages' themselves for others to read.

Each conference has its own "workspace" where participants can work collaboratively on a document/task.

CONVERSATIONS

Converstaions are closed and confidential private conferences Conversations allow small groups of people to correspond privately. Everyone in the group can see each others 'private' conversations.

MAIL

CoSy supports its own electronic mail system. You can send an electronic letter to any other CoSy user. Only that person can read such mail.

MODERATE

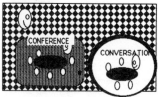

Any CoSy user can set up a new conference on a topic of interest to them. They can leave the conference OPEN for anyone to join and take part in, or they can make the conference CLOSED when participation will be by invitation only.

When you set up a conference, you take on the responsibility of MODERATING it. As Moderator, you have certain 'powers' over the conference and its partcipants.

Fig 16.4 — CoSy conferencing

```
Showing : 1. mail and conference status
          2. new messages
          3. partial listing of all available conferences
          4. joing a conference


              * * *   CoSy VMS v1.0   * * *

              Copyright University of Guelph
     Implemented by Disus, a Division of TSB International, Inc.
```

1
```
You have 0/83 mail message(s) in your in-basket,
You are a member of 37 conference(s)
        and 2 conversation(s).

No news is good news!
```

2
```
Conf/Topic                    New Messages
        bathgames/ispy            4
        d102bath/library          5
        database/database         7
        database/general          6
        database/instructions     40
           de304/course           1
     dt200-learn/go               1
     dt200-learn/junk             4
     dt200-lounge/lurk            18
     dt200-lounge/moans           11
     dt200-lounge/newconf         1
           glib/game              2
           glib/rules             1
          guest/guest             1
         itnews/block             1
         latest/info              32
           lurk/coming_out        12
           lurk/cosytips          24
```

3
```
:show all
o  3world          'Third World' issues
o  ai              Artificial Intelligence and all that Jazz
o  augustan        Group writing
o  basic2          Programs for GEM w/ Basic2
o  bathgames       Games and arenas for the weary
c  bathlearn       Bath University Conference on learning to learn
c  bathuni         A conference for Bath University Ed Tech Students
o  bboard          Bulletin Board
o  block1          For discussion of matters relating to block1 of dt
o  block5          DT200 Block 5 Manufacturing
o  block6          Block 6 DT200 Government
o  block7          messages about block 7 of dt200
o  communicate     The use of new communications media in Education
c  d102            Running Cosy at D102 Summer School
o  d102bath        d102 bath summer school conference
o  d103            For discussion of possible IT components in the ne
o  d309            D309
o  d421            course on on-line and CD-ROM searches
o  database        EXPERIMENTAL COSY DATABASE
o  de304           DE304 bulletin board
o  disabledpeople  Disabled Peoples International Centre support
c  dolcs           DOLCS Conference
```

4
```
:join bathlearn students

Joining conference 'bathlearn', topic 'students'. 0 new message(s) of 62.
```

*Fig 16.5 — Accessing CoSy, showing 1) mail and conference status 2) new message
3) partial listing of all available conferences 4) joining a conference*

example, obscene ones); can control entry to the conference (if it is a closed conference); can establish new topics in the conference, and so on.

The ability of computer mediated communications systems to support interactive group communications can be thought of in terms of a continuum of low to high group interaction, as is shown in Figure 16.6.

low ——————————————————————————— **high**

email   **bboards**   **computer conferencing**

Fig 16.6 — Group interaction

The Bath University trials
We have been using the CoSy system (on the Open University Vax computer at Walton Hall) at the University of Bath, School of Education in several trials of computer mediated communications. For example, Jack Whitehead has been running a conference on educational action research; the Values in Education Group has established a conference on values in education, and I have been using the system for seminar work with our MEd students, which I will discuss below.

Educational CC seminars
As part of the Educational Technology 2 module in the MEd course, students are introduced to new Information Technologies. We have begun to use CoSy, partly to introduce the students to a new example of Information Technology but mainly to conduct educational seminars via the medium. The trial is described elsewhere (McConnell, 1987a).

The seminar
Three separate conferences were established as part of the seminar trial:

1. A conference called Bathuni, set up with a topic for initial greetings by participants; a topic for news about the educational technology course; and a topic for users to provide feedback on the use of CoSy and about the seminar in general.

2. A conference called Bathgames, with two topics — a game of I Spy and a topic for general chit-chat.

3. A conference called Bathlearn. This was the main seminar conference, made up of a topic on student learning and another on experiential learning.

The conference lasted throughout the period of the Educational Technology 2 course, which was one term long (Spring, 1987). However, it occupied a relatively small part of the overall course.

Most students used terminals in the School of Education or University Computing Unit to access CoSy via the Joint Academic Network (JANET) service. Some had access to micros and modems at home or in their place of work, and linked-in via BT lines to the Open University national computer network. Eighteen students taking the course and the tutor took part in the seminar.

One of the aims of the trial was to examine the potential of computer conferencing for sustaining the quality and focus of conventional, face-to-face seminars. I was interested in the sort of discussions that take place over the medium and wanted to see if students truly conversed in a computer conference. Did they take up and follow points and issues raised by other participants in a conference, or merely add unassociated messages of their own to the conference?

What happens in a CC seminar?

I will focus here on the interactions that took place during the CC seminar and have a look at some of the discussions that evolved over time.

Interactions

Although our conferences took place during the Spring term, they still 'exist' on the CoSy system. By downloading the complete conference, it is possible to analyse the various forms of interaction that took place during the seminar.

Figure 16.7 (page 154) is a plot of the Learn topic in the Bathlearn conference (derived using the Ellis and McCreary [1985] method). The conference was concerned with student learning. We preceded the conference by reading one of Ference Marton's papers on student learning (Marton 1975). The first statement in the conference topic referred to Marton's work and set the context for the resulting discussion.

Several points can be made about this plot:

1. There are 62 statements in the topic. The lines indicate links between statements, which in turn indicate the path of discussions. Although the plot indicates a relatively uncomplicated set of interactions, statements would not be linked in this way if participants had been entering completely unassociated messages during the conference.

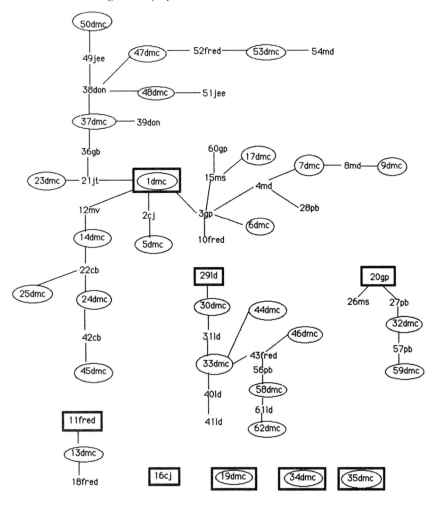

Fig 16.7 — Plot of Learn topic, conference Bathlearn

2. Out of the 62 statements in the topic, eight are 'freestanding' statements, ie they are unassociated messages. An unassociated message is one that does not relate directly to any other statement, or does not form a related comment to any other message.

    Statement 1 is an introduction to the conference, outlining its purpose, and was introduced by the moderator (dmc).

    Statements 11, 16, 20 and 29 were introduced by students.

    (Statements 19, 34 and 35 are news items about the course, and would have been better placed in the Bathuni conference, topic News.)

3. All of the remaining 53 statements are related comments, the lines indicating the paths of the relationships.

4. Clearly, more than one discussion took place during the conference. An analysis of the conference protocol suggests that there are seven different, but thematically related, discussions in this conference topic. These multiple simultaneous discussions took place over the length of the term and beyond (from January to May).

    Each discussion centres on different aspects of student learning, eg deep surface processing; adult and young people in learning, and so on.

    Each discussion is characterised by different groups of participants. However, it should be remembered that all participants could read all statements. The plot in Item 3 merely indicates those participants who actually entered a statement into the conference. Other participants could, of course, read these statements without actively participating in the discussion.

    Each discussion took place over differing time spans.

Discussions
An understanding of the content and quality of discussions requires an analysis of the statements in the discussion. As an example of this, we can look at the statements making up Discussion 7, beginning at statement 29 in Figure 16.7.

This discussion centred on two themes and was introduced by one of the students (statement 29). It began on 3rd March and concluded on 7th May (see Fig 16.8, page 156). The unedited transcript from this discussion is presented in the Appendix (page 165).

An analysis of the transcript shows the relationship of the statements and gives a summary of their content.

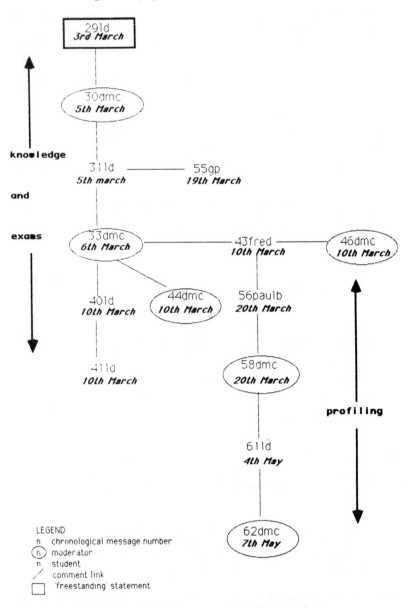

Fig 16.8 — Plot of group conversation over time

The first theme is a conversation between one of the students (1d) and the course tutor (dmc), and is about knowledge and exams (statements 29, 30, 31, 33, 40 and 41). (Statements 32 and 34 to 39 were entered in between and 'attached' as comments to other discussions — see the Plot in Figure 16.7.)

The second theme is a discussion about profiling, starting at statement 33.

Each statement in this discussion acknowledges the content of its predecessor. Points raised in one statement are taken up and developed or elaborated in other statements. For example, statement 33 (dmc) suggests that profiling might just be a way of substituting one form of control over students with another form. This point is taken up by Fred in statement 43, who elaborates it further by suggesting that the skills outlined in profiles might in fact lead to conformity, rather than individuality. Paulb, in statement 56, takes up this notion, saying that profiling might also extend control over parts of the syllabus not being examined.

Each participant was able to formulate their own statement in their own time and each statement, theoretically at least, had the same status as any other — it was there for all to read and consider on equal terms with any of the other statements. This allowed each student the opportunity to have what they wanted to say taken into account by the other participants: those who wanted to comment on it could do so, those who did not could just read it. This raises an interesting point about the democratic participatory nature of computer conferencing. All participants have the same opportunity to have their thoughts and ideas taken into account and listened to in a way that is often impossible in a face-to-face meeting (certainly with a class of 18 students).

Whether or not this actually happens in practice cannot be said from the present study. It is possible to skim over conference statements until you come to those entered by people you want to listen to or pay attention to (the header tells you who entered the statement). It is also possible to search a conference (by searching the headers and the text of statements and by using the 'reference' command which traces references to any particular statement throughout the conference) for particular themes and discussions that you only want to participate in. So, it is possible to ignore some participants, and to be ignored. For example, looking at the plot of the Learn topic in Figure 16.7, statements 2 and 11 were entered by students but were not actively taken up or commented on by other students (however, other students may well have read them and thought about their content without actively commenting on them, in a similar way to 'quiet' students who prefer not to participate in face-to-face sessions).

So, the medium has the potential for encouraging democratic participation in discussions; but whether or not this happens will depend on the way in which participants use it. In the correct educational context, with a democratic moderator, it can be hoped that this strength of the medium will emerge as a powerful educational tool.

In addition, because the conference statements are stored in the computer, it is possible to go over previously read statements to consider them again, or to reflect on their meaning in the light of experience. In these ways, a computer conference has the *potential* to encourage reflection and considered opinion, within a context in which participants actively pursue democratic participation.

Problems and constraints in participation
There are, of course, some problems and constraints for students in participating in educational seminars run via computer conferencing. This small-scale trial of computer conferencing as a seminar tool has indicated the following possible constraints.

The medium requires written statements. Research suggests that typing skills are not important for the success of computer conferences (Hiltz, 1984). Evaluation of this conference also suggests that is true (McConnell, 1987b). Nevertheless, when asked if they ever felt constrained in the type of contributions they could make, most students said they did feel constrained at some time. It could well be that, for some at least, having to present their thoughts publicly in typewritten form acted as a barrier to full participation. However, most of them said they were usually able to express their views during the conference.

As time goes on, the number of statements entered increases. Students reviewing a conference, or coming back to it after a period of absence, can be faced with many statements to consider and think about. This information overload can be a daunting phenomenon and can easily put them off. Most students said they felt 'overloaded' with information at some time during this conference. However, with increased expertise in the use of computer conferencing, it does become possible to manage the conference environment in ways which make the learning experience efficient and enjoyable. Having said that, we still do not know about the best ways in which to manage learning via conferencing (Harasim, 1987), nor do we know how learners in reality use the system. We can only learn about this by researching into the educational uses of the medium.

There are pressures of thinking on-line. In this trial, there were no facilities for students to download conference items for printing out, nor could many students prepare entries off-line to upload to the conference. So, all comments were made on-line, either directly after reading a statement, or sometime afterwards when the student had taken time to think about their comments. This clearly acted as a constraint on some students, either in them being unable to think on-line or being unable to prepare a message in direct response to another conference entry while on-line. Clearly, the provision of up-loading and down-loading facilities and printers would enhance the experience enormously.

Computer conferencing and group communications in education
This trial of computer conferencing has helped me understand the possibilities of the medium for carrying out group communications. What can, tentatively, be said about computer conferencing and group communications in education?

Group discussions
1. Everyone can read individual messages and follow the discussions taking place in a computer conference.

2. Participants can review the development of a discussion from the initial statement through all related statements.

3. Everyone can participate by adding statements of their own.

4. Those who do want to participate actively can still read what others say and benefit from that.

Group work
1. There is the potential for groups of learners to work co-operatively

   a) within a general conference
   b) by forming their own conference(s)
   c) by setting up private group conversations.

   However, this will only be effective if the focus is on the education *process* (Hiltz and Turoff, 1987) and not on the *product*.

2. Groups can work co-operatively on assignments/projects and the like, using CC as the medium of communication.

The democratic process
1. Students can take the lead in determining the focus, content and purpose of an educational computer conference. This can occur through students setting up their own conferences to discuss topics of their own interest; and in tutor-led discussions, by them taking advantage of the conferencing system which allows everyone the opportunity to say what they want to say. (Harasim, 1987b, also supports this view.)

2.   The medium has the potential of sustaining the individuality and autonomy of participants within a life-world validating discourse (Boyd, 1987; Whitehead and Lomax, 1987). Everyone has the same opportunity to input something on an equal basis, tutor and student alike. This is then permanently recorded for all other participants to read and consider.

3.   There is some indication that participants are more forthright in what they say in a computer conference than in face-to-face situations. In this respect, computer conferencing may act as an emancipatory medium.

Applications
Educational action research
In their paper 'Action Research and the Politics of Educational Knowledge', Whitehead and Lomax (1987) argue for a form of dialogue in action research that retains the autonomy of individuals:

'We claim that the logic of question and answer enables individuals to retain autonomy in relation to a body of knowledge about practice that remains relevant and valid' (p182).

They go on to describe by example a dialectical form of enquiry which is governed by question and answer. Their example is presented in the written form on paper; a debate between Jack Whitehead and Pam Lomax to which the reader is audience, not participant. Their concern is, however, to involve the reader as participant. Indeed, they finish their paper by leaving the debate open for others to participate in:

'Pam: Perhaps this is a good point at which to pause and invite others to join our dialogue?

Jack: Agreed. Who should we invite?

Pam: The BERA membership.'

It is not difficult to imagine this dialogue continuing electronically via a computer conference in which anyone (with suitable equipment) could participate. As we have seen, there is the possibility for the autonomy of the individual to be kept intact in a computer conference due to the democratic nature of the medium. Discussion can be by question and answer, rather than by purely propositional forms of knowledge and discussion. The medium seems to have potential for conducting educational action research as described by Whitehead and Lomax. Jack Whitehead's conference on Educational Action Research on the CoSy system has been experimenting with the medium in this respect.

Boyd (1987) also refers to the possibilities of the medium for supporting 'legitimative discourse':

'. . . it occurred to me when I came across Habermas, that perhaps computer-mediated teleconferencing is a medium through which his ideal discourse conditions can (very nearly) be met. . . . This is so because everyone can be given equal opportunity to enter arguments in the conference, and also because a moderator system can hide illegal entries from view. Threats and promises and rhetorical tricks can be archived, and dragged up after the main decisions have been taken if there is a challenge, but they can be kept out of immediate effect. It is crucial for liberative, life-world legitimating discourse that a centralised computer-mediating moderating conferencing system be used and not just exchanges of electronic mail. This is so, not only because illegal statements can be kept from influencing judgements, but in order that a permanent time-stamped archive of all transactions exist and be publicly accessible.' (Boyd, 1987 p169.)

INSET and distance learning
Computer conferencing, and computer mediated communications generally, can have a useful role to play in INSET and distance learning. The recent changes in INSET provision, away from college/university based INSET to school based INSET, and the changes in funding attached to this, suggest a role for computer conferencing. In-service education, which has been established with the co-operation of a college/university within the teachers' own institution, can be extended and developed via computer conferencing, keeping teacher and tutor in contact, and keeping teacher and teacher in contact as well. The in-service work can continue electronically, with teachers being supported at a distance.

It is also possible to see a role for computer conferencing as a means of peer group learning and exchange of information about practice. Teachers in one institution geographically isolated from another can interact and support each other; those experienced in certain aspects of the curriculum can act as a support and means of dissemination of ideas for others. The medium also seems to have great potential for group problem solving activities (Beckwith, 1987), an aspect which might well prove important in co-operative curriculum design across institutions and in the sphere of inter-class communications where students are working towards co-operative learning strategies.

Computer conferencing can also be a medium for the direct provision of courses for teachers. Many LEAs and teachers claim that there is insufficient time available for teachers to leave their institutions and travel to colleges/universities to take part in higher degree courses. And, in some

LEAs where additional cover is required for such 'absent' teachers, there is the additional cost involved. Where teachers are willing, computer conferencing could help overcome some of these difficulties. Teachers could study at a distance electronically at times (and places) most suitable to them. Additional cover would not be required since the teacher would still be available for classroom work — although such a scheme would benefit from the teacher being given some time off for study. However, such a system would be economically beneficial to those funding it — no loss of the teacher from the institution; no additional cover required; no travelling expenses to the college/university needed — all still within an environment which has been shown to be supportive to educational aims. This form of teacher education has been successfully used in Canada and elsewhere (for example, see the 'Canadian Journal of Educational Communication', 16(2), 1987 which is a special issue on computer mediated communication in education). The direct provision of educational courses by electronic means is in itself not new. The New Jersey Institute of Technology has been offering courses electronically worldwide for several years.

Such a scheme would, of course, have to address the problem of the provision of the equipment needed. Although most schools have a micro and modem, it would not be wise to assume that teacher(s) could have access to them for these purposes within the institution. Taking them home to use is equally problematic. Requiring students to own, or have ready access to, the necessary equipment would pose serious problems of equity. Perhaps the best scenario would be one in which the college/university loaned out to participating students all the equipment needed, to be used solely by them in their home for the duration of the course.

Conclusion
In this paper, I have attempted to give an indication of what happens in an educational computer conference.

A case study of the use of computer conferencing in an educational seminar has been discussed in order to indicate the potential of the medium for supporting interactive group communications. Although useful in illuminating some of the issues involved in educational computer conferencing, the case study is clearly limited in scope and educational focus. We need to conduct many more case studies which focus on the educational practice involved in computer conferencing in a wide variety of contexts so as to gain a greater understanding of the potential of the medium.

However, I feel that the quality of educational experience in an educational computer conference is potentially sufficiently good for us to accept the medium as a means of future educational communication and as a method for the direct provision of educational courses.

Acknowledgements
I would like to acknowledge the co-operation and participation of the students who took the Educational Technology 2 course, 1987, in the School of Education, University of Bath, and Tony Kaye of the Open University for making it possible to use the CoSy system on the OU Vax machine.

References and further reading
Beckwith, D (1987), Group Problem Solving via Computer Conferencing: the Realizable Potential, *Canadian Journal of Educational Communication, 16,* 2, Spring 1987.

Boyd, G (1987), Emancipative Educational Technology, *Canadian Journal of Educational Communication, 16,* 2, Spring 1987.

Brochet, M (1985), *Computer Conferencing as a Seminar Tool: a Case Study,* Workshop on Computer Conferencing, University of Guelph, Ontario, January 1985.

Canadian Journal of Educational Communication, 16, 2, Spring 1987 Special Issue, Computer Mediated Communication.

Ellis, M L and McCreary, E K (1985), *The Structure of Message Sequences in Computer Conferences: a comparative case study,* Workshop on Computer Conferencing, University of Guelph, Ontario, January 1985.

Emms, J and McConnell, D (1987), *An Evaluation of Tutorial Support Provided by Electronic Mail and Computer Conferencing,* 22nd Annual Conference of the Association for Education and Training Technology, University of Southampton, April 1987 (to be published in *Aspects of Educational Technology XXI,* forthcoming).

Harasim, L (1987a), *Computer Mediated Cooperation in Education: Group Learning Networks,* Second Symposium on Computer Conferencing, University of Guelph, Ontario, June 1987.

Harasim, L (1987b), Teaching and Learning On-line: Issues in Computer Mediated Graduate Courses, *Canadian Journal of Educational Communication, 16,* 2, Spring 1987.

Hiltz, S R and Turoff, M (1987), Workshop on CMC at the University of Guelph, Ontario, June 1987.

Hiltz, S R and Turoff, M (1987), *The Network Nation: Human Communication via Computers,* Addison Wesley, Reading, Mass.

Hiltz, S R (1984), *Online Communities: A Case Study of the Office of the Future,* Ablex Pub Co, Norwood, New Jersey.

Johansen, Valle, R J and Spangles, K (1979), *Electronic Meetings: Technical Alternatives and Social Choices,* Addison Wesley, Reading, Mass.

Kerr, E B (1986), Electronic Leadership: a Guide to Moderating Conferences, *IEE 'Transactions on Professional Communications Vol PC 29,* No 1 (March).

Kiesler, S, Siegal, J and McGuire, T W (1984), Social Psychological Aspects of Computer Mediated Communication, *American Psychologist,* October 1984.

Marton, F (1975), What Does It Take to Learn? in Entwhistle, N and Hounsell, D (eds), *How Students Learn, Readings in Higher Education 1,* University of Lancaster.

McConnell, D (1987a), *Computer Conferencing in the Development of Teacher Inservice Education,* Second Guelph Symposium on Computer Conferencing, University of Guelph, Ontario, June 1987. To be published in the *World Yearbook of Education, 1988: Education for the New Technologies.*

McConnell, D (1987b), *Use of the CoSy Computer Conferencing System as a Seminar Tool,* in the Educational Technology 2 Course at Bath University. Report prepared for the Computer Conferencing Group at the Open University. (Mimeo, School of Education, University of Bath, Bath, England.)

University of Guelph, *Compendium of University of Guelph Papers on Computer Conferencing, 1985-1987,* University of Guelph, Ontario, Canada.

University of Guelph, *Proceedings of First Symposium on Computer Conferencing, 1985,* University of Guelph, Ontario, Canada.

University of Guelph, *Proceedings of Second Symposium on Computer Conferencing, June 1987,* University of Guelph, Ontario, Canada.

Vivian, V (1986), Electronic Mail in a Children's Distance Course: Trial and Evaluation, *Distance Education 7,* 2.

Whitehead, J and Lomax, P (1987), Action Research and the Politics of Educational Knowledge, *British Educational Research Journal 13,* 2.

Appendix

Unedited transcript of group conversation in topic *Students,* conference *Bathlearn*

```
: join bathlearn students

Joining conference 'bathlearn', topic 'students'. 0 new message(s) of 62.

No more unread messages in this topic
Hit <RETURN> for next active conf/topic.
Read:29
============================
bathlearn/students £29,lynned, 414 chars,  3-MAR-87 17:18
There is/are comment(s) on this message.
----------------------------
TITLE: What pupils really learn about learning.
"...English is not history and history is not science and science
is not art and art is not music and art and music are minor subjects
and English, history and science major subjects, and a subject is something
youtake and, when you have taken it, you have 'had' it and if you have 'had'
it, you are immune and need not take it again" (Postman & Weingartner,1971).

No more unread messages in this topic
Hit <RETURN> for next active conf/topic.
Read:30
============================
bathlearn/students £30,dmc, 945 chars,  5-MAR-87 10:25
This is a comment to message 29
There is/are comment(s) on this message.
----------------------------
This is a typical conception of schooling and the acqusition of knowledge.
I think the problem lies partly in the concept of SUBJECTS - Ed Tech,
Curriculum Studies, Sociology - all ways of defining 'knowledege', packaging
it so leading to the attitude that once you've taken it, you've DONE it!

The focus is obviously wrong. There is nothing wrong with learning about
any of these topics in itself - but it is the relationship to the learner
that is surely vital. We see schoolong/education as being the accumulation
of knowledge about these subject areas; the focus shouls more be on the
learner and her needs and interests and where she is going, rather than
on what we can cram into his mind, how we can define the context and agenda
for learning. Holt and others have been writing about this for years - the
issue is clearly a political one. You have to fight for change. Our schools
and education system generally are controlling agents.

No more unread messages in this topic
Hit <RETURN> for next active conf/topic.
Read:31
============================
bathlearn/students £31,lynned, 731 chars,  5-MAR-87 16:35
This is a comment to message 30
There is/are comment(s) on this message.
----------------------------
The problem rests with an examination system. Examination qualifications are
currency! A commodity view of knowledge is thus inevitable. The answer is
abolish examinations and replace them with a system of profiling! There, I've
said it!
Through profiling there is a greater emphasis on cross curricular skills.
Asoects of the affective curriculum are relevant. The boundaries which exist
in
the school curriculum between subjects would become less defined. Ability
in certain areas of the curriculum would not be accredited with such high
status. Empires would crash! Learning for its own sake would become more
important than learning to pass an exam.. Its the difference between education
for life and training for occupation.
```

```
No more unread messages in this topic
Hit <RETURN> for next active conf/topic.
Read:33
===========================
bathlearn/students £33,dmc, 230 chars, 6-MAR-87 14:20
This is a comment to message 31
There is/are comment(s) on this message.
There are additional comments to message 31.
---------------------------
Are there not also problems with profiling in that you are substituting
one form of control over the students with another form, albeit one that
does try to give an overall portrayal of the students abilities and
accomplishments?


No more unread messages in this topic
Hit <RETURN> for next active conf/topik.
Read:40 ─────
===========================
bathlearn/students £40,lynned, 238 chars, 10-MAR-87 11:28
This is a comment to message 33
There is/are comment(s) on this message.
There are additional comments to message 33.
---------------------------
There are certainly some problems of a 'sociological' nature with
profiling. Broadfoot, 1986, suggests that it could become
 s seeming objectivity. Is that what you mean by control? Or are you
implying a sort of disciplinary framework?


No more unread messages in this topic
Hit <RETURN> for next active conf/topic.
Read:41
===========================
bathlearn/students £41,lynned, 311 chars, 10-MAR-87 11:38
This is a comment to message 40
---------------------------
Please ignore message no. 40. The machine 'gobbled up' a line of my text.
 Naughty machine! Broadfoot suggested that profiling could become a sort of
 'benign
surveillance' of pupils which would be all the more powerful for its
appatent objectivity. I7m not quite sure what you mean by control in this
 context.

No more unread messages in this topic
Hit <RETURN> for next active conf/topic.
Read:44
===========================
bathlearn/students £44,dmc, 265 chars, 10-MAR-87 22:46
This is a comment to message 33
---------------------------
I was thinking of control over the student in terms of being the person who
says whether they have achieved or not, carried out work according to set
criteria, shown accpetable behaviours etc.  Does profiling INVOLVE THE STUDENT
in defining the criteria/goals etc?


No more unread messages in this topic
Hit <RETURN> for next active conf/topic.
Read:55
===========================
bathlearn/students £55,georgep, 253 chars, 19-MAR-87 22:44
This is a comment to message 31
---------------------------
While I agree that profiling would relieve the situation to some degree I
do not think it would be the total answer.
It requires as I think Dave said in an earlier comment a much more
fundamental review of the way the whole learning process is
managed.
```

No more unread messages in this topic
Hit <RETURN> for next active conf/topic.
Read:43
===========================
bathlearn/students £43,fred, 865 chars, 10-MAR-87 12:43
This is a comment to message 33
There is/are comment(s) on this message.
There are additional comments to message 33.

Yes, the profile could easily be substituted for the exam as a new
form of tyranny. Just as educational practice is currently dominated
by the constraints of the examination system,so I could envisage a situation in
 whichwhat we do in the classroom is dictated by the desire to 'cover this
aspect of the profiles'. Indeed, I think this is already going on, and I
have probably been guilty of it when teaching on various BTEC courses
which require profiling. Those who provide these syllabi surely see the
profile as a means of ensuring teacher conformity to the norms which they
have set. It might be argued that the interpersonal and social skills
outlined in the profiles are designed to foster indiviuuality in the
learning process, yet even these 'skills' are conceived of in a rather
rigid sense in which conformity rather than individuality is rewarded.

No more unread messages in this topic
Hit <RETURN> for next active conf/topic.
Read:46
===========================
bathlearn/students £46,dmc, 373 chars, 10-MAR-87 22:54
This is a comment to message 43
There are additional comments to message 43.

Yes, it poses the question of who should be involved in designing the prifile
form. I think if the student can be involved then there is a better chance of
them understanding what is involved and appreciating it - their involvement
would also help to overcome the problem of conforming, by both the teacher
and the student.
But then, maybe thats a major role of profiling?

No more unread messages in this topic
Hit <RETURN> for next active conf/topic.
Read:56
===========================
bathlearn/students £56,paulb, 787 chars, 20-MAR-87 09:40
This is a comment to message 43
There is/are comment(s) on this message.

Taking up the notion of interpersonal and social skill profiles rewarding
conformity rather than individuality - is it fair to say that profiling
is a way of extending control over those areas that exams can't reach?
I feel that profiling is often an impertinence, in that one seeks to
measure what isn't being offered. Unless there is a radical change in
climate, students will feel threatened and alienated, and then we'll
penalise them for displaying a perfectly sensible response to their
situation. Which is not to say I'm against profiling, but I don't much
like the notion of teachers as untrained psychiatrists and social
workers. If our system remains fundamentally competitive, judgmental,
conformist and fear-based, what does it matter whether we have
profiles or exams?

No more unread messages in this topic
Hit <RETURN> for next active conf/topic.
Read:58
============================
bathlearn/students £58,dmc, 492 chars, 20-MAR-87 11:56
This is a comment to message 56
There is/are comment(s) on this message.   .

Yes, there does have to be a re-think about what schools are trying to
encourage students to do and be - the climate does have to change for
prfiling to be an imporatant factor - otherwise, as you say, there will
be an even greater tyranny and greater conformity in the pursuance of
trying to please teachers in EVERYTHING students do because EVERYTHING
they do is to be 'assessed'.

I would be interested to hear what the rest of you think about Paul's
points. Are you there Lynne??

David

No more unread messages in this topic
Hit <RETURN> for next active conf/topic.
Read:61
============================
bathlearn/students £61,lynned, 814 chars, 4-MAY-87 13:33
This is a comment to message 58
There is/are comment(s) on this message.

Yes, David, I'm here. I've read the previous comments with interest and I'm
 tempted to suggest that lack of research data, as yet, concerning the use of
profiling techniques and their 'currency' with pupils, parents, teachers
and employers should prevent us from being too pessimistic. My recent
attempts at piloting profiling as an integral feature of curriculum
design and teaching method would seem to indicate that pupils have an
increased desire to learn, brought about by the fact that they have
a greater say in what they learn, how they do it and how they are
assessed. Profiling appears to be providing the incentive for pupils
to take greater responsibility for their own learning. That in itself
is surely an improvement on the carrot/stick syndrome of an examination
system. 'q'

'quit'
'.<CR>'
.<CR>

No more unread messages in this topic
Hit <RETURN> for next active conf/topic.
Read:62
============================
bathlearn/students £62,dmc, 283 chars, 7-MAY-87 17:52
This is a comment to message 61

Yes indeed Lynne, that all sounds very worthwhile for the students involved.
We certainly do need some research into the effectiveness etc of profiling.
How about doing an MPhil on it?!!